Interdisciplinary and Intercultural Programmes in Higher Education

This book is designed to make visible how the logic-in-use of researchers leads to particular understandings of phenomena of interest (such as opportunities for learning specific processes) and shapes a particular view of what evidence counts in constructing warranted claims. The contributions brought together here invite readers to explore the processes involved in developing and studying educational innovations, and to undercover the interdependent conceptual and epistemological actions, processes and practices of instructors, programme developers and students.

Taken together, the book brings forward an argument related to the reflexive turn – the understanding that researchers in the social sciences construct, rather than find, phenomena of interest. Therefore, this book creates the potential to examine not only the logic-in-use developed by different researchers, but also to examine the complex nature of particular phenomena of interest to the researcher themselves. This book was originally published as a special issue of *Pedagogies: An International Journal*.

Judith L. Green is the Professor Emeritus in the Department of Education at the University of California, Santa Barbara, USA.

W. Douglas Baker is a Professor in the Department of English Language and Literature at Eastern Michigan University, Ypsilanti, USA.

Interdisciplinary and Intercultural Programmes in Higher Education
Exploring Challenges in Designing and Teaching

Edited by
Judith L. Green and W. Douglas Baker

LONDON AND NEW YORK

First published 2017
by Routledge
2 Park Square, Milton Park, Abingdon, Oxon, OX14 4RN, UK

and by Routledge
711 Third Avenue, New York, NY 10017, USA

Routledge is an imprint of the Taylor & Francis Group, an informa business

© 2017 Taylor & Francis

All rights reserved. No part of this book may be reprinted or reproduced or utilised in any form or by any electronic, mechanical, or other means, now known or hereafter invented, including photocopying and recording, or in any information storage or retrieval system, without permission in writing from the publishers.

Trademark notice: Product or corporate names may be trademarks or registered trademarks, and are used only for identification and explanation without intent to infringe.

British Library Cataloguing in Publication Data
A catalogue record for this book is available from the British Library

ISBN 13: 978-1-138-70110-6

Typeset in TimesNewRomanPS
by diacriTech, Chennai

Publisher's Note
The publisher accepts responsibility for any inconsistencies that may have arisen during the conversion of this book from journal articles to book chapters, namely the possible inclusion of journal terminology.

Disclaimer
Every effort has been made to contact copyright holders for their permission to reprint material in this book. The publishers would be grateful to hear from any copyright holder who is not here acknowledged and will undertake to rectify any errors or omissions in future editions of this book.

Contents

Citation Information   vii
Notes on Contributors   ix

Introduction: Exploring challenges in designing and teaching
(inter)disciplinary and (inter)cultural programmes in higher education   1
W. Douglas Baker and Judith L. Green

1. Language and culture learning in higher education via telecollaboration   5
Dorothy M. Chun

2. An emic lens into online learning environments in PBL in undergraduate dentistry   22
Susan Bridges

3. Designing interdisciplinary instruction: exploring disciplinary and conceptual differences as a resource   38
W. Douglas Baker and Elisabeth Däumer

4. Challenging points of contact among supervisor, mentor teacher and teacher candidates: conflicting institutional expectations   54
Laurie Katz and Zeynep Isik-Ercan

5. Navigating across academic contexts: Campo and Angolan students in a Brazilian university   70
Maria Lucia Castanheira, Brian V. Street and Gilcinei Teodoro Carvalho

6. Interdisciplinary dialogues as a site for reflexive exploration of conceptual understandings of teaching–learning relationships   86
Judith L. Green, Yun Dai, Jenna Joo, Edward Williams, Ang Liu and Stephen C.-Y. Lu

Index   105

Citation Information

The chapters in this book were originally published in *Pedagogies: An International Journal*, volume 10, issue 1 (January–March 2015). When citing this material, please use the original page numbering for each article, as follows:

Introduction
Exploring challenges in designing and teaching (inter)disciplinary and (inter)cultural programmes in higher education
W. Douglas Baker and Judith L. Green
Pedagogies: An International Journal, volume 10, issue 1 (January–March 2015) pp. 1–4

Chapter 1
Language and culture learning in higher education via telecollaboration
Dorothy M. Chun
Pedagogies: An International Journal, volume 10, issue 1 (January–March 2015) pp. 5–21

Chapter 2
An emic lens into online learning environments in PBL in undergraduate dentistry
Susan Bridges
Pedagogies: An International Journal, volume 10, issue 1 (January–March 2015) pp. 22–37

Chapter 3
Designing interdisciplinary instruction: exploring disciplinary and conceptual differences as a resource
W. Douglas Baker and Elisabeth Däumer
Pedagogies: An International Journal, volume 10, issue 1 (January–March 2015) pp. 38–53

Chapter 4
Challenging points of contact among supervisor, mentor teacher and teacher candidates: conflicting institutional expectations
Laurie Katz and Zeynep Isik-Ercan
Pedagogies: An International Journal, volume 10, issue 1 (January–March 2015) pp. 54–69

CITATION INFORMATION

Chapter 5
Navigating across academic contexts: Campo and Angolan students in a Brazilian university
Maria Lucia Castanheira, Brian V. Street and Gilcinei Teodoro Carvalho
Pedagogies: An International Journal, volume 10, issue 1 (January–March 2015) pp. 70–85

Chapter 6
Interdisciplinary dialogues as a site for reflexive exploration of conceptual understandings of teaching–learning relationships
Judith L. Green, Yun Dai, Jenna Joo, Edward Williams, Ang Liu and Stephen C.-Y. Lu
Pedagogies: An International Journal, volume 10, issue 1 (January–March 2015) pp. 86–103

For any permission-related enquiries please visit:
http://www.tandfonline.com/page/help/permissions

Notes on Contributors

W. Douglas Baker is a Professor in the Department of English Language and Literature at Eastern Michigan University, Ypsilanti, USA.

Susan Bridges is an Associate Professor in the Centre for the Enhancement of Teaching and Learning Faculty at the University of Hong Kong.

Gilcinei Teodoro Carvalho is a Professor in the Department of Teaching Methods and Techniques at the Federal University of Minas Gerais, Belo Horizonte, Brazil.

Maria Lucia Castanheira is a Professor in the Department of Teaching Methods and Techniques at the Federal University of Minas Gerais, Belo Horizonte, Brazil.

Dorothy M. Chun is a Professor of Applied Linguistics and Education at the University of California, Santa Barbara, USA.

Yun Dai is a Ph.D. student in the Graduate School of Education at the University of California, Santa Barbara, USA.

Elisabeth Däumer is a Professor of English and Women's and Gender Studies at Eastern Michigan University, Ypsilanti, USA.

Judith L. Green is the Professor Emeritus in the Department of Education at the University of California, Santa Barbara, USA.

Zeynep Isik-Ercan is an Associate Professor and Program Coordinator of Early Childhood Education at Rowan University, Glassboro, USA.

Jenna Joo is a Ph.D., Research Analyst and Assistant to the Dean of Continuing Education at the University of California, Santa Barbara, USA.

Laurie Katz is a Professor in the Department of Teaching and Learning at Ohio State University, Columbus, USA.

Ang Liu is a Senior Lecturer and Director of Engineering Design, School of Mechanical and Manufacturing Engineering, University of New South Wales, Australia.

Stephen C.-Y. Lu is a Professor in the Department of Industrial and Systems Engineering at the University of Southern California, Los Angeles, USA.

Brian V. Street is the Professor Emeritus and Chair of Language in Education at King's College London, UK.

Edward Williams is a Ph.D. student in Teaching and Learning at the University of California, Santa Barbara, USA.

INTRODUCTION

Exploring challenges in designing and teaching (inter)disciplinary and (inter)cultural programmes in higher education

The articles of this special issue are grounded in a series of epistemological dialogues among the authors over the past two decades. At the centre of these dialogues has been the exploration of how the logic-in-use (Birdwhistell, 1977) constructed for a study leads to particular understanding of the phenomena of interest (e.g., opportunities for learning specific processes and practices required within and across disciplines). Additionally, these dialogues have explored how a particular logic-in-use shapes a particular view of what counts as evidence as well as what evidence counts in constructing warranted claims.[1] In bringing these articles together, our goal was two-fold. Our first goal was to invite readers into these dialogues by creating opportunities to examine not only what the researchers found but also the often-invisible processes involved in developing and studying educational innovations-in-the-making, i.e., the conceptual and epistemological processes involved in developing new approaches, or in transforming previously held institutional, programmatic and (inter)disciplinary perspectives.

Our second goal was to make possible the exploration of the complex, multi-perspective, multi-faceted and multi-level analyses that the authors viewed as necessary to uncover a series of interdependent conceptual and epistemological actions, processes and practices of instructors, programme developers and students. As each article reveals, these logics-in-use were undertaken to develop understanding of the consequential nature of what was being made available to students within and across times in particular classrooms (e.g., Castanheira, Crawford, Dixon, & Green, 2000; Green, Skukauskaite, & Baker, 2012) as well as to their instructors/advisors/supervisors in particular educational settings. This volume makes possible exploration of the logics of inquiry that the different authors constructed to explore the opportunities for learning that were being developed in particular (inter)institutional, (inter)disciplinary and/or (inter)national contexts.

Together, these articles, and the dialogues with the editors in which they are embedded, can be understood as bringing forward arguments related to the *reflexive turn* in the Social Sciences. This turn has led to the understanding that researchers, grounded in particular disciplines and theoretical traditions, *construct*, not *find*, the phenomena of interest.[2] From this perspective, we view these articles as creating a potential for examining the logic-in-use developed by different authors, or research teams, in order to examine the complex nature of particular phenomena of interest to the author(s). Readers of this special issue, therefore, are invited to explore the particular languages (theories) underlying this collection of studies and how these languages frame the phenomena of interest, the questions studied, the methodologies used to collect, analyse and construct data, as well as the ways of constructing warranted accounts from these epistemological decisions and actions (cf., Kelly, 2006). These dialogues are related to recent calls for transparency in reporting research (e.g., American Educational Research Association, 2006) necessary to enable readers across traditions, disciplines and national contexts to interpret and understand the diverse bodies of research.

The articles as telling cases

One way to understand each article is to view it as a *telling case* (Mitchell, 1984), which traces both developing understanding of fundamental phenomena in particular fields and the logic-of-inquiry that the authors developed to study such phenomena in classrooms and other educational settings. These articles make transparent how the authors engaged in the process that Mitchell framed as *analytic induction*. In these studies, therefore, the focus is not on a site, a group or a problem, as is often the case in other forms of case studies (e.g., illustrative of theory, descriptive of a setting or group, or representative of particular processes, actors, or others). Thus, a telling case can be viewed as one in which "the events themselves may relate to any level of social organization: a whole society, some section of a community, a family or an individual" (p. 238).

From this perspective, we view a classroom, a discipline and a university setting as socially organized, and not merely as an existing structure that predefines what counts as learning, pedagogy or disciplinary knowledge. In each telling case, the authors explore "the particularity of the circumstances surrounding any case or situation (or set of situations)" (p. 241) and make visible how the particularity of the case is located within some wider setting or context, a condition that Mitchell argues is necessary in constructing a telling case. For each study, the particularity being examined is one related to pedagogical decisions in classrooms as well as the challenges facing the students and their instructors (and others), as they engage with, and plan for ways of developing, and at times, transforming the opportunities for learning for particular groups of students within and across disciplines and (inter)national contexts.

Across the telling cases, readers are invited to examine how authors brought different theoretical perspectives to bear on particular pedagogical and broader contextual phenomena (e.g., personal, social, disciplinary and institutional programme histories), and how their logic-in-use framed a basis for uncovering social, cultural, linguistic and conceptual factors that informed, supported and/or constrained discursive interactions among participants, and through these analyses how they identified potential consequences of those interactions for student and instructor learning and actions. Each of the authors, therefore, offers a telling case that reveals a range of theoretical and epistemological processes needed to uncover previously invisible factors related to both the research process and the accounts possible through such processes. Across the articles, readers will also be able to explore unanticipated challenges that students as well as designers (instructors, advisors, and supervisors) faced in creating and/or participating in innovative opportunities for learning particular processes as well as knowledge within, and in some instances, across disciplines and national contexts.

A closing and an opening

We conclude this introduction with one additional framework that supports exploration of different programmes of research and their *expressive potential(s)*. While the discussion of transparency above has framed the need for exploring different articles, philosopher Kenneth Strike (1974, 1989) has taken this argument further in framing the concept of a *programme of research* as more than an individual study. He argues that a programme of research refers to a philosophical approach of a research community (e.g., behaviourism, social constructionism, constructivism and post-structuralism). He also has shown that within such communities, there are different ways of framing the work, from those adhering closely to the core conceptual arguments to those who adapt these in different ways to address problems of interest. He argues that each programme creates an *expressive potential* for both readers of the tradition and those within the particular programme that, if accepted, enable examination of the underlying logic of inquiry and epistemological process that constitute a particular programme of research:

- They provide the context in which theoretical and empirical terms are defined. Indeed, they provide the characterization of what is to count as a theoretical and an empirical term.
- They enable us to distinguish relevant from irrelevant phenomena. That is, they inform us as to what phenomena a given enterprise is expected to deal with. And they tell us what sorts of questions are appropriate to ask about them.
- They provide the perceptual perspectives and categories by means of which the world is experienced. They tell us what is to count as a well-formed or appropriate account of phenomena–that some proposed accounts will be excluded at the outset because they are not properly structured or because they do not fulfill the conception of a proper account within the field.
- Through historical precedent or the logical outgrowth of the accepted assumptions, programs of research point toward the problems that require solution. A problem will be a conflict between the intellectual aspirations of a research program and its current capacity.
- They provide the standards of judgment – epistemological criteria – that we use to evaluate proposed accounts, and they tell us what is to count as evidence for proposed accounts. (Strike, 1989, p. 6)

We presented Strike's principles so that readers can explore the expressive potential guiding the different articles that we view as constituting telling cases, which, when taken together, make visible a larger programme of research – sociocultural programme of research grounded in social constructionist perspectives on the nature of social reality. Although the authors do not directly reference this perspective in their articles, a social constructionist perspective on sociocultural theories has been part of our ongoing dialogues that is exploring epistemological and conceptual bases of our common research programme. Thus, by applying Strike's principles in reading these different articles, readers will be able to explore the expressive potential not only of the individual articles but also how across the articles, researchers were able to uncover often invisible dimensions of complex programmes. In this way, readers will be able to identify what can be learned by such systematic analyses of the conceptual underpinnings of the logic-in-use of the different authors, and how these telling cases create a basis for developing a more complex understanding of how moments of instruction are made available (or not) to diverse groups of students in emerging and complex learning contexts.

Notes

1. For examples of recent volumes exploring the nature of evidence, see Luke, Green, and Kelly (2006, 2010) for articles across multiple levels nationally and internationally and Moss (2007) for the nature of evidence across different research traditions. For discussion of limits to certainty in interpreting and reporting accounts, see Baker and Green (2007) and Heap (1980).
2. For a historical development of these and related arguments across disciplines, see Clifford and Marcus (1986) in Anthropology, Patai (1988) in Folklore, Atkinson (1990) in Sociology and Bucholtz (2000) in Applied Linguistics. For how to examine the expressive potential of

different programmes of research in Education, see Bredo (2006), Kelly (2006), and Strike (1974, 1989).

References

American Educational Research Association. (2006). Standards for reporting on empirical social science research in American Educational Research Association (AERA) publications. *Educational Researcher, 35*(6), 33–40. doi:10.3102/0013189X035006033

Atkinson, P. (1990). *The ethnographic imagination: Textual constructions of reality.* London: Routledge.

Baker, W. D., & Green, J. L. (2007). Limits to certainty in interpreting video data: Interactional ethnography and disciplinary knowledge. *Pedagogies: An International Journal, 2*(3), 191–204. doi:10.1080/15544800701366613

Birdwhistell, R. L. (1977). Some discussion of ethnography, theory and method. In J. Brockman (Ed.), *About Bateson: Essays on Gregory Bateson* (pp. 103–144). New York, NY: E. P. Dutton.

Bredo, E. (2006). Philosophies of educational research. In J. L. Green, G. Camilli, & P. B. Elmore (Eds.), *Complementary methods in education research* (pp. 3–31). Mahwah, NJ: Lawrence Earlbaum (for AERA).

Bucholtz, M. (2000). The politics of transcription. *Journal of Pragmatics, 32*, 1439–1465. doi:10.1016/S0378-2166(99)00094-6

Castanheira, M. L., Crawford, T., Dixon, C., & Green, J. (2000). Interactional ethnography: An approach to studying the social construction of literate practices. *Linguistics and Education, 11*(4), 353–400. doi:10.1016/S0898-5898(00)00032-2

Clifford, J., & Marcus, G. E. (1986). *Writing culture: The poetics and politics of ethnography.* Berkeley: University of California.

Green, J. L., Skukauskaite, A., & Baker, W. D. (2012). Ethnography as epistemology: An introduction to educational ethnography. In J. Arthur, M. Waring, R. Coe, & L. V. Hedges (Eds.), *Research methodologies and methods in education.* London: Sage.

Heap, J. L. (1980). What counts as reading: Limits to certainty in assessment. *Curriculum Inquiry, 10*(3), 265–292. doi:10.2307/1179615

Kelly, G. (2006). Epistemology and educational research. In J. L. Green, G. Camilli, & P. B. Elmore (Eds.), *Complementary methods in education research* (pp. 31–53). Mahwah, NJ: Lawrence Earlbaum (for AERA).

Luke, A., Green, J., & Kelly, G. J. (Eds.). (2010). What counts as evidence and equity? In *Review of research in education* (Vol. 34). Thousand Oaks, CA: SAGE (AERA journal).

Mitchell, J. C. (1984). Typicality and the case study. In R. F. Ellen (Ed.), *Ethnographic research: A guide to general conduct* (pp. 238–241). New York, NY: Academic Press.

Moss, P. A. (Ed.). (2007) *Evidence and decision making: The 106th yearbook of the National Society for the Study of Education, Part I.* Malden, MA: Blackwell.

Patai, D. (1988). *Brazilian women speak: Contemporary life stories.* Princeton, NJ: Rutgers University.

Strike, K. A. (1974). On the expressive potential of behaviorist language. *American Educational Research Journal, 11*(2), 103–120. doi:10.3102/00028312011002103

Strike, K. A. (1989). *Liberal justice and the Marxist critique of education: A study of conflicting research programs.* New York, NY: Routledge.

W. Douglas Baker
Department of English Language and Literature, Eastern Michigan University, Ypsilanti, MI, USA

Judith L. Green
Department of Education, Gevirtz Graduate School of Education, University of California, Santa Barbara, CA, USA

Language and culture learning in higher education via telecollaboration

Dorothy M. Chun

Department of Education, University of California, Santa Barbara, USA

> This article focuses on the ways of researching the process of designing, developing, and using telecollaboration (also known as online intercultural exchange) to facilitate the learning of both linguistic and *intercultural communicative competence* (ICC) in higher education courses in different educational contexts in the United States, Europe, and Asia. Although telecollaboration would intuitively seem to be an ideal medium for learning another language and about another culture, extensive research has shown that this learning process takes years and faces many challenges. This paper situates the research on language and culture learning within the broader scope of language and intercultural education (see *Pedagogies, 8*(2), for a report of an interview with Michael Byram, one of the originators of the concept of ICC). A multinational example of the integration of telecollaborative networks in European university language classes collaborating online, the INTENT project, is described. In addition, a telling case, the *Cultura* model, implemented in the United States, Europe, and Asia, demonstrates a successful approach (with accompanying research) to telecollaboration for language and culture learning. However, there are also invisible factors and unanticipated challenges that teachers and learners need to understand in order to benefit from these telecollaborative environments; these are examined at the end of the article.

1. Introduction

In the most general sense, *telecollaboration* is the process of communicating and working with other people, individually or in groups, in different geographical locations through online or virtual means. Telecollaboration can be implemented in a variety of settings, e.g., in the case of higher education, in the classroom, in a computer lab, and at home, through the use of Web-based tools and resources, such as email, forums, blogs, wikis, text-chat, voice-chat, videoconferencing, and social networking sites. In the field of second language (SL) and foreign language (FL) learning in higher education, telecollaboration has been theorized most frequently from sociocultural perspectives and holds the potential to enrich the learning experience by providing SL/FL learners with opportunities for interaction and communication with others who know the same language.

For SL/FL educational activities, telecollaboration is often used synonymously with the term *online intercultural exchange* (OIE) (see O'Dowd, 2007). O'Dowd (2011) states that "traditionally, online intercultural exchange projects in foreign language education have involved the use of (text-based) online communication tools to bring together classes of language learners in different countries to learn the others' language and culture" (p. 369).

OIEs have generally taken one of two forms, firstly, the e-tandem model, and secondly, the blended intercultural model. In the e-tandem model, two native speakers of different languages communicate with the aim of learning the other's language. In these exchanges, which can be via synchronous modes (e.g., text-chat or video-chat) or asynchronous modes (e.g., email or wiki), learners provide feedback to their partners on content and language performance. The second model goes to great lengths to integrate the online interaction into the learners' language programs and often involves "international class-to-class partnerships in which projects and tasks are developed by the partner teachers in the collaborating institutions" (p. 370). Learning through OIE is gaining in popularity and is particularly widespread in higher education, as it is theorized to improve second/foreign language learners' linguistic and cultural knowledge of the SL/FL and increase their global awareness.

The goal of this paper is to provide an overview of the ways of researching the design, development and use of telecollaboration to facilitate the learning of both linguistic and intercultural communicative competence in higher education courses in different educational contexts globally. Although telecollaboration can be used for a wide range of purposes for the teaching and learning of many different subjects (a larger "global" perspective), this paper discusses "local" applications to SL/FL learning and teaching. After reviewing the theories, research methodologies and selected current studies that report on language and culture learning outcomes, ways of researching the design and development of telecollaborative projects, are summarized. Finally, some of the invisible or less discussed factors that teachers and learners need to understand in order to benefit from these telecollaborative environments are examined. These issues are based primarily on OIEs that have been conducted in the United States, Europe, and Asia and reported in Chun (2014a).

The sub-field of telecollaboration for SL/FL learning is nearly two decades old, enabled by the World Wide Web. Warschauer (1996a) collected contributions to a symposium on Local and Global Electronic Networking in Foreign Language Learning and Research, which was held at the University of Hawai'i and which brought together educators concerned with these issues from universities and K-12 institutions throughout the world. At the time, most of the telecollaborative projects relied on email, threaded forum discussions, and other Web 1.0 capabilities. Since then, other edited volumes on Internet-mediated intercultural FL education have appeared (Belz & Thorne, 2006; Dooly & O'Dowd, 2012; Lamy & Hampel, 2007; O'Dowd, 2007). Guth and Helm's (2010) and Dooly and O'Dowd's (2012) volumes discussed the educational shift to Web 2.0 tools, such as synchronous chat, wikis, blogs, social networking, and 3D virtual worlds. Pertinent details from these volumes are discussed in the following sections.

2. Theories and methods used in research on FL/SL telecollaboration

The important publication edited by Dooly and O'Dowd (2012) synthesized many methods and theoretical approaches that have been and are being used to investigate different configurations of FL/SL telecollaboration. They attribute the attention being paid by both educators and researchers to online interaction and exchange in FL education to three factors: (1) the growing emphasis in the FL/SL education community of the integral role of culture in FL/SL learning, and in particular, the recognition that online intercultural interaction can support the development of learners' cultural awareness and skills of *intercultural communicative competence* (ICC) proposed by Byram (1997) and defined below; (2) the rise of *sociocultural* theory as applied to FL/SL learning, viewing language acquisition as facilitated by carefully constructed, purposeful, communicative events; and (3) the way in which FL/SL competence and e-literacies have merged and become inextricably linked to learning, working, and living in the twenty-first century in general.

It may surprise some to note that the field of FL/SL education did not always emphasize the importance of teaching culture along with language. Agar (1994), a linguistic anthropologist, justifiably criticized the field of linguistics in the first half of the twentieth century for its narrow focus on the sound systems and grammars of languages that did not include the study of culture. The field of applied linguistics, which was established in part as a response to generative linguistics (late 1950s, 1960s), emerged as an interdisciplinary research field in the 1970s. Agar's (1994) concept of "languaculture" found resonance with Whorf's (1956) ideas; Agar agreed with Whorf that "studying language and studying culture *were the same thing* (italics in original)" (p. 71). Risager (2005) argues that languaculture (LC) is a key concept in language and culture teaching, and proposes that language and culture pedagogy focus on the "study of meaning as it is produced in the interface of languaculture and discourse" (p. 195).

Taking the close integration of language and culture a step further, Byram's (1997) use of the term "intercultural communicative competence" deliberately maintained the link with the term "communicative competence" which gained importance in FL teaching in the late 1970s. "Communicative competence" includes not only the traditional "grammatical competence" but also "sociolinguistic/pragmatic competence," "discourse competence," and "strategic competence" (Canale, 1983; Hymes, 1972) emphasizing the fact that in order to communicate, language learners not only need grammatical skills and knowledge but also social knowledge about how and when to use utterances appropriately. Byram extended the competence requirements even further, theorizing about the complexity of ICC. An interculturally competent speaker is able to effectively exchange information with members of the target culture and does so by displaying attitudes of curiosity and openness, demonstrating the knowledge of how language and culture are related in the target culture, possessing skills of interpreting and relating, and being able to use, in real-time conversations, an appropriate combination of knowledge, skills, and attitudes to interact with speakers from a different country or culture.

In the American and European context, many applied linguists have argued that language and culture must be treated as inseparable constructs (Kramsch, 1993). Recent work focuses on the pedagogies that seek to develop intercultural competence; for example, Byrnes (2009) examines three documents produced by the Council of Europe and two US national organizations, ACTFL (American Association of Teachers of Foreign Languages) and MLA (Modern Language Association): (1) the *Common European Framework of Reference* (CEFR; Council of Europe, 2001), (2) the *Standards for Foreign Language Learning* (ACTFL, 2006), and (3) the report by the Modern Language Association Ad Hoc Committee on Foreign Languages (2007) entitled "Foreign Languages and Higher Education: New Structures for a Changed World." All of these national (US) and multinational (European) guidelines indicate a shifting emphasis toward the important role of culture in the FL/SL profession. Each of the documents "assumes that language use must be seen as embedded in diverse social activities in the lives of people and peoples around the globe" (p. 316) and advocates that the goal of FL/SL education is to develop speakers who have deep translingual and transcultural competence. With the focus on the learning of language and culture together, the great majority of studies discussed in the following sections have addressed both and not only language (see Reinhardt, 2012). However, we begin with theories of second language acquisition

(SLA) and broaden the scope to include theorizations of the acquisition of cultural knowledge and ICC.

2.1 Underlying theories and appropriate methodologies

The theoretical bases for studies of telecollaboration for language and culture learning are interdisciplinary, culled from theories of SLA and theories of intercultural education. In fact, in the digital age, it has become the norm to advocate and theorize about multiple e-literacies (multi-literacies) in many, if not all, areas of learning. In SL/FL learning in particular, as multilingualism and globalization are increasing, ICC is directly linked to working and functioning in the world (Dooly & O'Dowd, 2012). Dooly and Hauck (2012) propose the need for research on multi-modal communicative competence (MCC), as daily interactions in formal and informal language learning have increasingly switched to online modes, e.g., audio- and videoconferencing.

One of the historical dichotomies in SLA research is the cognitive–social divide, i.e., the long-standing debate on whether to focus on the *psychological* aspects of language acquisition as opposed to the *social* aspects of learning, which in turn influences both what is considered the appropriate object and method of investigation. In general, studies based on a *cognitive* framework tend to select experimental, psychometric methods, while those based on *sociocultural* frameworks tend to prefer the use of qualitative and ethnographic methods. In practice, though, many studies adapt and combine frameworks and methods, e.g., *socio-cognitive* approaches, blurring the traditional dichotomy. This section presents representative studies employing the various frameworks and methods. Table 1 provides an overview of the main theories or models and the relative importance of language vs. culture in FL/SL education.

Table 1. Theories and models of SLA and development of ICC.

Theory/model	Perspective	Conceptual principle	Relative importance of language vs. culture
Psycholinguistic/ cognitive	Linguistic competence	Grammatical aspects of language can be learned cognitively, by instruction	Language more important
Sociocultural/ social	Communicative competence	Social interaction is key to language acquisition	Focus on social, contextual, and cultural factors in L2 learning and use
ICC/rich points in LC1 and LC2	Critical cultural awareness; dynamic, heterogeneous view of culture	Dimensions of knowledge, skills, attitudes, and beliefs (of both language and culture)	Language and culture equally important; concept of LC "languaculture"
Ecological	Broad perspective of studying organisms in their relations with their environment	*Affordances* (tools in the learner's environment) and *scaffolding*	Focus on naturalistic contexts, with language and culture equally important

INTERDISCIPLINARY AND INTERCULTURAL PROGRAMMES

2.1.1 Cognitive and psycholinguistic theories of SLA

One of the main theoretical frameworks on the cognitive side is the *input–interactionist* paradigm (Long, 1996), and the early research on online interaction in FL/SL contexts focused on the development of linguistic competence in in-class interaction, e.g., comparing online synchronous interaction with face-to-face student interaction. Many of these studies used a quantitative methodology, involving control groups of students engaged in face-to-face interaction that were compared to experimental groups of learners participating in online interaction or intra-class studies in which the same students took part in both face-to-face and online interaction (Warschauer, 1996b). What was often counted and categorized were linguistic features and language functions (e.g., Chun, 1994; Kern, 1995), and researchers showed how negotiation for meaning occurs in intra-class online chat (e.g., Blake, 2000). Similarly, studies of online interaction based on *psycholinguistic* theories of SLA (e.g., Ellis' (2006) Associative Cognitive CREED and Schmidt's (1990) Noticing Hypothesis) have found that text-based chat promotes noticing of grammatical and lexical features or errors (e.g., Lai & Zhao, 2006; Lee, 2008). Other studies of inter-class interactions between learners and native speakers (Tudini, 2003) or tandem learning partnerships (Kötter, 2003; O'Rourke, 2005) have investigated form-focused interaction, negotiation of meaning and code switching, primarily linguistic aspects of SL/FL learning.

2.1.2 Sociocultural theories of SLA

In contrast to interactionist research, Block (2003) proposed the "social turn" taken by the field of SLA, and variations of socially based theories and approaches have flourished. For example, *socio-cognitive* paradigms (Kern & Warschauer, 2000), which view language as social and place emphasis on the role of cultural context and discourse, are often used in the research on telecollaboration. Many studies have been influenced by *sociocultural* theory (Belz, 2002; Thorne, 2003; Ware, 2005). In the Vygotskian perspective, language is viewed as a mediating tool for learning, and the entire language learning process must by necessity be a dialogic process (see, e.g., Basharina, 2007; Blin, 2012, who rely on Activity Theory and Cultural Historical Activity Theory, respectively, for their analyses of telecollaboration).

Other studies make visible the development of linguistic, pragmatic, and intercultural competence in both intra-class telecollaboration (e.g., Abrams, 2008) and inter-class interactions (e.g., Belz & Thorne, 2006; Jin & Erben, 2007). Chun (2011) reports on advanced German learners in the United States engaging online with advanced English learners in Germany, as they used different types of speech acts to indicate their pragmatic ability and to show their developing ICC. Specifically, some learners realized that they could exhibit curiosity and interest (a component of ICC) by engaging in multi-turn statements and did not need to use questions to convey their intent.

2.1.3 Intercultural communicative competence

The research at the nexus of sociocultural learning and online exchange has often focused on the development of *intercultural communicative competence* or ICC (Byram, 1997; Chun, 2011; O'Dowd, 2003) and on the instances of intercultural misunderstanding and occasional conflict in online interaction (O'Dowd & Ritter, 2006; Ware & Kramsch, 2005). These misunderstandings and conflicts are examples of Agar's (2006) "rich points," defined as "those surprises, those departures from an outsider's expectations that signal differences between LC1 [languaculture 1] and LC2 [languaculture 2] and give direction to subsequent learning" (p. 2). For these socioculturally oriented studies, the methodology used is generally qualitative in nature. For example, Ware (2005) explored the online interactions between advanced-level learners of English in Germany and advanced-level students of German in the United States using qualitative methods to analyse online transcripts, interviews, and questionnaires, and focusing on the factors that led to "missed communication."

2.1.4 *Ecological approaches*

In both SLA and CALL (computer-assisted language learning) research, a new perspective may be found in *ecological* approaches, e.g., van Lier (2004), who takes an ecological world view and applies it to language education. Ecology broadly studies organisms in their relations with their environment. Van Lier's approach thus incorporates many different perspectives with regard to language learning, e.g., sociocultural theory, semiotics, ecological psychology, and the concepts of self and identity. Key constructs in this approach to language learning are *affordances* and *scaffolding*, with an affordance defined as the relationship between an organism and something in the environment that can potentially be useful for that organism. Technology is viewed as a source of affordances and learning opportunities for language learners. Appropriate scaffolding, i.e., help from peers, teachers, or technology itself, might also be necessary, and this is a core feature of telecollaboration.

2.2 *Methodologies for researching telecollaboration*

Research on telecollaboration and OIE appears to be moving from studying the end products of exchanges, e.g., more quantitative analyses of email, forum discussion, chat, to examining the processes of exchanges, and how cultural meanings are expressed, e.g., more qualitative, contextualized, discourse-based analyses of what participants produce over time. Processes and meanings are not readily measurable in typical quantitative studies, e.g., with rigorous, experimental study designs, which measure quantity or frequency; rather, qualitative studies are better suited to interpretative approaches of longitudinal data. In addition, since telecollaboration can take place both inside and outside of traditional classrooms, it is not feasible to control for all of the variables that might influence an exchange, thus making the use of qualitative research methodologies more appropriate (Levy & Stockwell, 2006; Müller-Hartmann, 2000).

A reasonable alternative is to use multiple methods, as all research methods have inherent strengths and limitations, and triangulation of different methods can compensate for the weaknesses to a certain extent. For language acquisition research, Dörnyei (2007) suggests that quantitative and qualitative methods are not mutually exclusive, and that combining them offers multiple epistemologies within each type. Certainly for virtual, intercultural, and multimodal FL/SL research contexts, multi-method approaches can be advantageous because each partner in an exchange represents a unique situation and the types of interaction can be varied, resulting in multiple forms of multimodal data. In addition, particularly with the development of ICC, two factors must be considered: first, developing ICC is a continuous, multi-step endeavour that ideally requires months, if not years; and second, online activities that contribute to the development of ICC cannot be separated from classroom-based activities, as follow-up in face-to-face classroom discussion of telecollaborative interactions has been shown to be crucial (see Chun, 2014a; Chun & Wade, 2004; Furstenberg & Levet, 2014).

Ware and Rivas (2012) provide an overview of mixed method research designs for online exchanges, discussing examples to date, and acknowledging that these exchanges can be seen through multiple lenses, allowing for different types and levels of analysis (Liaw, 2006; Liaw & Bunn-LeMaster, 2010).

In a study of an intercultural learning project between ELF (English as Lingua Franca) students in France and Taiwan, Liaw and English (2014) employed mixed methods to analyse their data. The goal of the project was to foster participants' awareness of cultural identities and the knowledge of *self* and *otherness*. Qualitatively, the Lacanian concept of *extimacy* and Bakhtin's concept of *exotopia* formed the basis to analyse the writing produced by their students.

Quantitative analyses were performed with a text analysis software program, Linguistic Inquiry and Word Count (LIWC) (Pennebaker, Francis, & Booth, 2001). Specifically, the number of social process words written by the two groups of students was tracked, and the statistical analyses revealed that the Taiwanese students' use of social process words (referring to family, friends, and other people) was significantly higher than that of the French participants, suggesting that the students in Taiwan had "a higher degree of interpersonal connectedness and personal-emotional identification with the messages they wrote" (p. 81).

Finally, in addition to the traditional quantitative and qualitative methods, Dooly and Hauck (2012) suggest that *action research* can also be considered by self-reflective teachers in order to improve their own practices and to gain more insight into the learning process. Müller-Hartmann (2012) provides detailed discussions of how to implement a case study approach using action research and how activity theory can help the researcher deal with the rich contextualized data in telecollaboration.

In summary, past research on language and culture learning in higher education of FL/SL learning has been based on a variety of underlying theories of SLA, employing both quantitative and qualitative methodologies. However, the current trend of having ICC as one of the primary goals of telecollaboration has motivated many researchers to take sociocultural approaches and utilize multiple methodologies, including action research. The following section discusses research on the design and development of telecollaborative exchanges.

3. A telling case: researching the development of telecollaboration in different global educational contexts

Michael Byram, "one of the main international referents in intercultural education" (Porto, 2013, p. 143), was a plenary speaker at the recent international conference in 2014 on "Telecollaboration in University Foreign Language Education" at the University of León, Spain, which aimed to bring together educators, researchers, mobility coordinators, and university management interested in exploring the integration of OIE projects at universities around the globe (http://unicollaboration.unileon.es/). The conference was part of a larger project, the INTENT project (Integrating Telecollaborative Networks into Foreign Language Higher Education), which has been funded by the European Commission since 2011 (Guth, Helm, & O'Dowd, 2012).

The broad array of presentations at the conference demonstrated the wide variety of ways in which online exchanges can be implemented and can contribute not only to second/foreign language learning and intercultural awareness, but also to general educational goals, internationalization of education, and electronic/digital literacies in higher education (see http://unicollaboration.unileon.es/downloads/detailed_conference_programme.pdf). Of the 75 presentations at the conference, including three plenaries, one-third of them dealt with telecollaboration that was focused on goals and issues larger than language and culture learning, while two-thirds were concerned specifically with the teaching and learning of foreign/second language and culture.

Among the presentations at the 2014 INTENT conference that focused specifically on or targeted language and culture learning, the *Cultura* model stood out as one of a select few that has enjoyed impressive longevity and reach in terms of successful models of telecollaboration. In this section of the paper, the focus is thus on a "telling case," how research on *Cultura*-based projects in different global settings has been conducted, summarizing (1) the *Cultura* model, (2) a meta-synthesis of *Cultura*-inspired projects, and (3) the development of three *Cultura*-based projects in different global education contexts.

3.1 The Cultura *model*

The *Cultura* model was developed by Furstenberg, Levet, English, and Maillet (2001) and is based on the premise that language and culture are inextricably connected and on a view of culture as a dynamic, ever-evolving process of expressing both individual and collective identities, world views, ethics, morals, and values. As such, culture cannot be "taught" in the traditional sense of teachers imparting knowledge to students, but must be experienced by the learners, as they co-construct cultural knowledge with others. Although their model was developed at the same time that Byram (1997) proposed the concept of ICC and was not based per se on ICC, their ideas certainly resonate with those of Byram. According to Byram (1997), ICC involves five elements: attitudes (of curiosity and openness), knowledge (of social groups and their products and practices), skills of interpreting and relating, skills of discovery and interaction, and critical cultural awareness.

Furstenberg and Levet (2014) reflect on possible reasons for the longevity of the model, and why it has been such a compelling and enduring prototype for online intercultural exchanges. The original exchange in 1997 involved a class of students at MIT who were learning French and students at the Ecole Supérieure d'Aéronautique in Toulouse, France, who were studying English. Asynchronous online forum discussions were the primary mode of interaction. Since then, numerous such exchanges have been conducted, and a wealth of captivating examples illustrate the discovery process that students go through in expanding and deepening their understanding of their own and the other culture. New technologies that have become available since 1997, e.g., videoconferencing, blogs, and wikis, have been used with the model, but it is not the tools that cause meaningful communication to happen; rather, it is important to choose the technologies that can best serve the goals of intercultural learning.

3.2 A meta-synthesis of Cultura-*based projects*

Due to the fact that the *Cultura* model has been adapted by dozens of other teachers and researchers, Chun (2014b) performed a meta-synthesis of such projects, extensively surveying 18 instructors who responded to a detailed questionnaire. This meta-synthesis is an example of how the design and development of telecollaborative projects can be researched. This type of research does not investigate specific language or ICC learning outcomes but can inform the development of future such telecollaborative projects.

With regard to the first research question of the meta-synthesis, "What were the goals that led to the adoption of the *Cultura* model and what were the outcomes that the *Cultura* model might achieve?", the respondents believed that the *Cultura* model would increase their students' language skills and their confidence and motivation for communicating in the SL/FL. Furthermore, they hoped for an improvement in their students' awareness and openness to another culture as well as cultural knowledge and the skills of analysis, abstraction, reflection, exploration, and sharing. The majority of the survey respondents taught in 4-year universities around the world (American Samoa, Canada, France, Germany, Italy, Japan, Spain, Taiwan, the United States), almost half of them taught English, and most students were intermediate or advanced SL/FL learners.

Results of the meta-synthesis with respect to the second research question, "What were the processes in the implementation of the project that built toward the goals?", revealed that there was great variability in implementation. Interestingly, most of the projects were only a relatively small part of the language curriculum, and in some cases, they were extracurricular or optional activities. This is in fact the opposite of what is done in the Furstenberg et al. (2001) model, in which the online *Cultura* exchange forms the basis for the entire curriculum, and face-to-face discussions in the classroom are predominantly about the content posted online. Among the 18 survey respondents, approximately 90% of them used word associations and sentence completions in their exchanges (see Appendix A for examples), and text-based chat, text-based forums, and video chats were the most widely used modes of interaction. In addition, and very importantly, the great majority of projects used a combination of online activities with partners and face-to-face discussions in the classroom. Teachers' participation in the online activities was minimal for the most part, and the length of the exchanges ranged from 3 to 24 weeks, again reflecting a wide range of how the exchanges were realized.

The responses to the third research question, "What kind of data was gathered in order to determine whether the goals were achieved, and how do the data reflect the types of learning outcomes that were addressed and assessed in the *Cultura* project?", revealed that a wide variety of data were gathered, both online and offline. In addition to the online data produced during the exchanges (postings in questionnaires, forums, text chats, wikis, blogs, and videoconferences), offline data included class presentations and discussions, learner diaries, worksheets, essays, reflective reports, self-assessments, and post-project surveys and interviews. Although a greater number of survey responders had privileged cultural gains over linguistic gains at the start of their projects, they cited almost as many gains in linguistic skills, knowledge, and attitudes as gains in cultural skills, knowledge, and attitudes as outcomes at the end of the projects. This meta-synthesis provided a number of recommendations for future projects, and they are presented in the Conclusions section of this paper.

3.3 Selected Cultura-inspired exchanges in different global contexts

The first sample project is Liaw and English's (2014) intercultural learning project between ELF students in France and Taiwan. Liaw and English designed a task-based telecollaboration in which students engaged in various types of multimodal, computer-mediated exchanges. Their goal was to develop communication skills via asynchronous text, graphic, and audio-video exchanges, and the study provides an excellent example of research on the design, development, and use of telecollaboration. Based on their experiences in designing and implementing their exchange, they recommend careful planning of tasks in order to direct students' attention to meaningful and purposeful interaction. In their experience, making culture the focus of discussions allowed students to have a voice in the exchange as "experts" in their own very different cultures and to speak their own minds.

A second example to illustrate design, development, and implementation of a *Cultura* exchange is the China-USA Business Café (CUBC) project reported by Jiang, Wang, and Tschudi (2014) between students at the University of Hawai'i and Tianjin Foreign Trade Vocational College with a goal of fostering the cultural component of students' communicative competence in Chinese. The teaching model adopted in CUBC is based on *Cultura* and emphasizes cross-cultural learning through exploration and discovery, consisting of the following five steps: (1) accessing authentic cultural material, (2) posting personal responses to the material, (3) observing and analysing others' responses to the material, (4) engaging in exchange and discussion based on one's analysis, and (5) self-reflection.

The word association task and subsequent follow up online discussion demonstrated that through comparative analysis and discussion of concrete examples, students came to recognize that the "same" word in different cultures may represent a completely different concept: words that appear to be translations or glosses of one another may have quite different semantic fields in different cultures.

A third project based on the *Cultura* model used a design and implementation similar to the CUBC described above but differed in that it involved primarily heritage learners of Filipino. Domingo (2014) reports on the Filipino Heritage Language Café, whose goals were (1) to improve and enhance intermediate Filipino language learners' language proficiency and cultural competence; (2) to create a learning environment in cyberspace that would expand student awareness of a community of learners and provide a forum to examine Filipino identity and culture, and (3) to enable students to compare and experience Filipino culture vicariously from another perspective and geographic location.

Two implementations of the online Café involved learners studying Filipino at universities in the United States, and one iteration was an exchange between two US universities and the University of the Philippines. In the exchanges, students first introduced themselves to each other online, then filled out word associations and sentence completions, typical of *Cultura*-based projects, and subsequently discussed the results of the word associations and sentence completions in online forums.

Analyses of the forum postings that were made revealed concrete evidence that students were able to synthesize that they had read in the others' postings and to hypothesize about why their fellow students wrote what they did, which was one of the key expectations of the instructors. Students appreciated the fact that in the word association and sentence completion activities, they were the experts in their own culture, and the multiplicity of voices and knowledge expressed in the forums surpassed what they might have learned from only their teacher's perspective.

To summarize, this section has presented a widely used model of telecollaboration for language and culture learning (the *Cultura* model). Selected studies on the design, development, and implementation of the model in different global contexts have shown the model's strengths and affordances. But there are also some limitations and invisible constraints in telecollaborative projects which are discussed in the following section.

4. Invisible factors in telecollaboration implementation and research

As attested by the previous sections, telecollaboration and OIEs have been very successful, both for language and culture learning in different higher education contexts. Successes include personal and cultural benefits, linguistic and sociolinguistic improvements, development of intercultural communication skills, and critical cultural awareness raising. However, there are less visible dimensions that warrant discussion, and they are the focus of this section.

In a review of studies on telecollaborative exchanges, O'Dowd and Ritter (2006) discovered many examples of "failed communication," when online intercultural exchanges did not result in successful communication or negotiation of meaning between the learners. They developed an inventory of factors that could lead to cases of so-called failed communication, divided into four levels: individual, classroom, socioinstitutional, and interaction. For example, teachers who do not have institutional support or have different curricular goals or requirements than their partners often find it difficult to devote time to such exchanges. Interaction factors included "the misunderstandings and tension which arise from cultural differences in communicative style and behavior" (p. 634). Similarly, Lamy and Goodfellow (2010) ascribe difficulties, tensions, and failure of telecollaborative projects to a wide variety of factors, e.g., negative transfer, differences in negotiation or interactional "styles," professional misalignments, practical constraints, teacher workload, and conflicting world views.

Based on the different kinds of research discussed in this paper, three main types of constraints are proposed, constituting some so-called invisible factors that teachers and researchers should be aware of when developing, implementing, and researching online intercultural exchanges.

4.1 Constraints of technology

Thorne (2003) presented three telling case studies of OIEs and found that computer users from different cultures had different views on which technologies were appropriate for the exchange. For example, he reported on a generational shift in communication tool preference, discovering that a ubiquitous tool, email, was unsuitable for mediating peer relationships among undergraduate university students (in the United States and France) who were engaged in an intercultural exchange. Email was found to be constraining, whereas instant messaging was found to be a more appropriate tool for interpersonal peer relationship building. Thorne therefore suggested that the medium, i.e., the technological tools, is not a neutral factor in OIEs.

Chun (2011) also found in her study with advanced learners of German in the United States that the US students were not satisfied with only using text-chats but would have preferred video-chats with their telecollaborative partners in Germany. At the time of the exchange, videoconferencing was not available on campus for students, exemplifying a technological constraint.

On a related issue regarding methodological constraints, Smith's (2008) study of a computer-mediated communication (CMC) environment for language learning found that looking only at the final product of text-chat logs misses important processes of self-repairs in the language learning process. By examining the screen capture videos of the entire chat interaction, which had become feasible technologically, he was therefore able to show fundamentally different features of the interactional data. This makes visible that at any given point in time, technologies have certain affordances but also inherent constraints.

4.2 Constraints of the configuration

As many of the studies discussed in this paper and Chun's (2014a) collection of studies on OIEs have found, there are numerous organizational, institutional, and curricular issues that contribute to difficulties or less successful telecollaborative projects, specifically challenges with scheduling, differences in time zones and lengths of the exchange, and differences in project goals due to curricular and institutional constraints.

O'Dowd (2011), for example, noted that short-term exchanges can actually have more negative than positive consequences on learners' intercultural awareness. Jiang et al. (2014) found in their CUBC project that not all aspects of their exchange were coordinated and monitored continuously by both partner teachers, including time coordination, teaching and student training, operating procedures, and performance objectives and expectations. In terms of curricular issues, Domingo (2014) suggested that some of the challenges of the Filipino Heritage Café were due to the fact that the online exchange was not an integral part of the curriculum.

4.3 Constraints of the learners and the learning context

Challenges in telecollaborative projects that can be attributed to the learners themselves and the learning contexts and assumptions surrounding them include differences in linguistic proficiencies among the partner classes, willingness of learners to write honestly and openly, cultural differences and conflicts, and the possibility of reinforcing preconceptions and stereotypes of the learners. It is important to note, though, as Lamy and Goodfellow (2010) did, that the field of telecollaboration has moved "from the notion of 'conflict as accidental finding of research' to 'conflict as object of research'" (p. 109). This resonates with Agar's (2006) concept of rich points, and he suggests "Those moments of incomprehension and unmet expectations are the fuel that drives ethnographic research" (p. 5).

For example, Chun and Wade's (2004) students stated to their instructors (during class time) that they did not always express their honest thoughts and feelings in the online exchange and that they felt that their partners were not "interested" in them or their opinions because they did not ask many questions. Their online postings were friendly and positive, without a hint of any discontent. In the CUBC project, Jiang et al. (2014) found that the two classes were not well matched in terms of linguistic proficiency, and therefore the American students were not always able to understand the colloquial written language produced by their partners.

4.4 Constraints of the teachers' role

Although Furstenberg and Levet (2014) advise that teachers not intervene in the online parts of the exchanges, they certainly believe that the teachers' role is important for planning and follow-up purposes. Belz (2003) and O'Dowd and Ritter (2006) have emphasized that the points of tensions in intercultural exchanges should not categorically be avoided, but rather that such differences should be used as rich points to explain and discuss cultural contexts and practices that learners could analyse and make conscious efforts to understand. Similarly, Schneider and von der Emde (2006) view conflict as a learning opportunity. It is therefore critical for the teacher to follow up on these points in the classroom (see O'Dowd, 2013).

Ware and Kramsch (2005) described an extended episode of misunderstanding between two students (one who was learning German in the United States and the other who was learning English in Germany) during an asynchronous telecollaborative project. Communication breakdowns online can make visible the pragmatic assumptions that are generally taken for granted (speech acts, conversational maxims, facework). Learners are often unaware of these assumptions, particularly when conversing in a second language, and it is therefore essential for teachers to help students go beyond comprehending the surface meaning of words and sentences in order to understand what their intercultural partners are writing.

5. Conclusions and recommendations

With regard to selecting a theoretical basis and research methodology for studying telecollaborative projects, broader theories that take social communication into account (as opposed to the primarily linguistic or psycholinguistic theories) are preferable since ICC necessarily involves and is dependent upon human interaction. As such, socio-cognitive, sociocultural, and ecological approaches (including ethnographic and action research) lend themselves better to understanding and explaining authentic interactions. Accordingly, solely quantitative methodologies are not able to capture the complex nuances of intercultural discourse and thus qualitative methods or, alternatively, multiple methods are more appropriate for this type of research, analysing not only online interactions but also ethnographic data, interview, and questionnaire data, as well as teacher/researcher observations.

Telecollaboration can be instrumental in language and culture learning, awareness raising, highlighting rich points, and development of ICC by providing learners with a variety of opportunities for both linguistic and cultural experiences. However, simply connecting learners with each other online does not ensure a successful intercultural exchange. Based on the research presented in this paper and on Chun's (2014b) meta-synthesis, unanticipated challenges, divided by O'Dowd and Ritter (2006) into four levels (individual, classroom, socioinstitutional, and interactional), arise not infrequently. The various constraints due to technology, curricular timeframes and issues, the learners and the learning context, and the role of the teacher suggest that future research approaches must consider these constraints and integrate them into the design of their methodologies.

With regard to design and development of telecollaborative projects or online intercultural exchanges, teachers need to (1) be realistic about the goals and what is achievable with their specific learners and the learners' level of proficiency; (2) carefully plan every aspect of the exchange, from discussing the goals with both partner teachers and students, to agreeing on similar assignments and curricular integration, to training the learners to use the technology appropriately; (3) adapt whichever model of exchange they choose to follow to their (and their students') particular needs and goals; (4) resolutely follow up on the students' online exchanges in the classroom so that misunderstandings can be resolved and reinforcing of stereotypes can be avoided. This attention to the invisible or unanticipated challenges, along with selecting an appropriate research methodology, might allow us to progress in our understanding of intercultural programs in higher education.

References

Abrams, Z. I. (2008). Sociopragmatic features of learner-to-learner computer-mediated communication. *CALICO Journal, 26*(1), 1–27.

ACTFL. (2006). *Standards for foreign language learning in the 21st century* (3rd ed.). Yonkers, NY: National Standards in Foreign Language Education Project.

Agar, M. (1994). *Language shock: Understanding the culture of conversation*. New York, NY: William Morrow and Company.

Agar, M. (2006). Culture: Can you take it anywhere? *International Journal of Qualitative Methods, 5*(2), 1–16.

Basharina, O. (2007). An activity theory perspective on student-reported contradictions in international telecollaboration. *Language Learning & Technology, 11*(2), 36–58.

Belz, J. A. (2002). Social dimensions of telecollaborative foreign language study. *Language Learning & Technology, 6*(1), 60–81.

Belz, J. A. (2003). Linguistic perspectives on the development of intercultural competence in telecollaboration. *Language Learning & Technology, 7*(2), 68–117.

Belz, J. A., & Thorne, S. (2006). Internet-mediated intercultural foreign language education and the intercultural speaker. In J. A. Belz, & S. L. Thorne (Eds.), *Internet-mediated intercultural foreign language education* (pp. viii–xxv). Boston, MA: Heinle & Heinle.

Blake, R. (2000). Computer mediated communication: A window on L2 Spanish interlanguage. *Language Learning & Technology, 4*(1), 120–136.

Blin, F. (2012). Introducing cultural historical activity theory for researching CMC in foreign language education. In M. Dooly, & R. O'Dowd (Eds.), *Researching online foreign language interaction and exchange* (pp. 79–106). Bern: Peter Lang.

Block, D. (2003). *The social turn in second language acquisition*. Washington, DC: Georgetown University Press.

Byram, M. (1997). *Teaching and assessing intercultural communicative competence*. Clevedon: Multilingual Matters.

Byrnes, H. (2009). Revisiting the role of culture in the foreign language curriculum. *The Modern Language Journal, 94*(2), 315–336. doi:10.1111/j.1540-4781.2010.01023.x

Canale, M. (1983). From communicative competence to communicative language pedagogy. In J. C. Richards, & R. W. Schmidt (Eds.), *Language and communication* (pp. 2–27). London: Longman.

Chun, D. M. (1994). Using computer networking to facilitate the acquisition of interactive competence. *System: An Interactive Journal of Educational Technology and Applied Linguistics, 22*(1), 17–31. doi:10.1016/0346-251X(94)90037-X

Chun, D. M. (2011). Developing intercultural communicative competence through online exchanges. *CALICO Journal, 28*(2), 392–419. doi:10.11139/cj.28.2.392-419

Chun, D. M. (Ed.). (2014a). *Cultura-inspired intercultural exchanges: Focus on Asian and Pacific languages*. Honolulu, HI: University of Hawaii, National Foreign Language Resource Center.

Chun, D. M. (2014b). A meta-synthesis of Cultura-based projects. In D. M. Chun (Ed.), *Cultura-inspired intercultural exchanges: Focus on Asian and Pacific languages* (pp. 33–63). Honolulu, HI: University of Hawaii, National Foreign Language Resource Center.

Chun, D. M., & Wade, E. R. (2004). Collaborative cultural exchanges with CMC. In L. Lomicka, & J. Cooke-Plagwitz (Eds.), *Teaching with technology* (pp. 220–247). Boston, MA: Heinle.

Council of Europe. (2001). *Common European Framework of Reference for languages: Learning, teaching, assessment*. Cambridge: Cambridge University Press.

Domingo, N. P. (2014). UHM-UCLA Filipino Heritage Café and the Fil-Ams quest for identity. In D. M. Chun (Ed.), *Cultura-inspired intercultural exchanges: Focus on Asian and Pacific*

languages (pp. 139–155). Honolulu, HI: University of Hawaii, National Foreign Language Resource Center.
Dooly, M., & Hauck, M. (2012). Researching multimodal communicative competence in video and audio telecollaborative encounters. In M. Dooly, & R. O'Dowd (Eds.), *Researching online foreign language interaction and exchange* (pp. 135–161). Bern: Peter Lang.
Dooly, M., & O'Dowd, R. (Eds.). (2012). *Researching online foreign language interaction and exchange*. Bern: Peter Lang.
Dörnyei, Z. (2007). *Research methods in applied linguistics: Quantitative, qualitative and mixed methodologies*. Oxford: Oxford University Press.
Ellis, N. C. (2006). Cognitive perspectives on SLA: The associative-cognitive CREED. *AILA Review, 19*, 100–121. doi:10.1075/aila.19.08ell
Furstenberg, G., & Levet, S. (2014). Cultura: From then to now. In D. M. Chun (Ed.), *Cultura-inspired intercultural exchanges: Focus on Asian and Pacific languages* (pp. 1–31). Honolulu, HI: University of Hawaii, National Foreign Language Resource Center.
Furstenberg, G., Levet, S., English, K., & Maillet, K. (2001). Giving a virtual voice to the silent language of culture: The *Cultura* project. *Language Learning & Technology, 5*(1), 55–102.
Guth, S., & Helm, F. (Eds.). (2010). *Telecollaboration 2.0: Language, literacy and intercultural learning in the 21st century*. Bern: Peter Lang.
Guth, S., Helm, F., & O'Dowd, R. (2012). University language classes collaboration online: A report on the integration of telecollaborative networks in European universities. Retrieved from http://intent-project.eu/intent-project.eu/sites/default/files/telecollaboration_report_final_oct2012.pdf
Hymes, D. H. (1972). On communicative competence. In J. B. Pride, & J. Holmes (Eds.), *Sociolinguistics: Selected readings* (pp. 269–293). Harmondsworth: Penguin.
Jiang, S., Wang, H., & Tschudi, S. (2014). Intercultural learning on the web: Reflections on practice. In D. M. Chun (Ed.), *Cultura-inspired intercultural exchanges: Focus on Asian and Pacific languages* (pp. 121–137). Honolulu, HI: University of Hawaii, National Foreign Language Resource Center.
Jin, L., & Erben, T. (2007). Intercultural learning via instant messenger interaction. *CALICO Journal, 24*(2), 291–311.
Kern, R. (1995). Restructuring classroom interaction with networked computers: Effects on quantity and characteristics of language production. *The Modern Language Journal, 79*, 457–476. doi:10.1111/j.1540-4781.1995.tb05445.x
Kern, R., & Warschauer, M. (2000). *Network-based language teaching: Concepts and practice*. Cambridge: Cambridge University Press.
Kötter, M. (2003). Negotiation of meaning and codeswitching in online tandems. *Language Learning & Technology, 7*(2), 145–172.
Kramsch, C. (1993). *Context and culture in language teaching*. Oxford: Oxford University Press.
Lai, C., & Zhao, Y. (2006). Noticing and text-based chat. *Language Learning & Technology, 10*(3), 102–120.
Lamy, M.-N., & Goodfellow, R. (2010). Telecollaboration and learning 2.0. In S. Guth, & F. Helm (Eds.), *Telecollaboration 2.0* (pp. 107–138). Bern: Peter Lang.
Lamy, M.-N., & Hampel, R. (2007). *Online communication in language teaching and learning*. Basingstoke: Palgrave McMillan.
Lee, L. (2008). Focus-on-form through collaborative scaffolding in expert-to-novice online interaction. *Language Learning & Technology, 12*(3), 53–72.
Levy, M., & Stockwell, G. (2006). *CALL dimensions: Options and issues in computer-assisted language learning*. Mahwah, NJ: Lawrence Erlbaum.
Liaw, M.-L. (2006). E-learning and the development of intercultural competence. *Language Learning & Technology, 10*(3), 49–64.
Liaw, M.-L., & Bunn-LeMaster, S. (2010). Understanding telecollaboration through an analysis of intercultural discourse. *Computer Assisted Language Learning, 23*(1), 21–40. doi:10.1080/09588220903467301
Liaw, M.-L., & English, K. (2014). A tale of two cultures. In D. M. Chun (Ed.), *Cultura-inspired intercultural exchanges: Focus on Asian and Pacific languages* (pp. 67–90). Honolulu, HI: University of Hawaii, National Foreign Language Resource Center.
Long, M. (1996). The role of the linguistic environment in second language acquisition. In W. Ritchie, & T. Bhatia (Eds.), *Handbook of second language acquisition* (pp. 413–468). San Diego, CA: Academic Press.

Modern Language Association Ad Hoc Committee on Foreign Languages (2007). Foreign languages and higher education: New structures for a changed world. *Profession, 2007*, 234–245. doi:10.1632/prof.2007.2007.1.234

Müller-Hartmann, A. (2000). The role of tasks in promoting intercultural learning in electronic learning networks. *Language Learning & Technology, 4*, 129–147.

Müller-Hartmann, A. (2012). The classroom-based action research paradigm in telecollaboration. In M. Dooly, & R. O'Dowd (Eds.), *Researching online foreign language interaction and exchange* (pp. 163–204). Bern: Peter Lang.

O'Dowd, R. (2003). Understanding the "other side": Intercultural learning in a Spanish-English e-mail exchange. *Language Learning & Technology, 7*(2), 118–144.

O'Dowd, R. (Ed.). (2007). *Online intercultural exchange: An introduction for foreign language teachers*. Clevedon: Multilingual Matters.

O'Dowd, R. (2011). Online foreign language interaction: Moving from the periphery to the core of foreign language education? *Language Teaching, 44*(3), 368–380. doi:10.1017/S0261444810000194

O'Dowd, R. (2013). The competences of the telecollaborative teacher. *The Language Learning Journal*. Advance online publication. doi:10.1080/09571736.2013.853374

O'Dowd, R., & Ritter, M. (2006). Understanding and working with "failed communication" in telecollaborative exchanges. *CALICO Journal, 23*(3), 623–642.

O'Rourke, B. (2005). Form-focused interaction in online tandem learning. *CALICO Journal, 22*(3), 433–466.

Pennebaker, J. W., Francis, M., & Booth, R. (2001). *Linguistic inquiry and word count: LIWC 2001*. Mahwah, NJ: Erlbaum.

Porto, M. (2013). Language and intercultural education: An interview with Michael Byram. *Pedagogies: An International Journal, 8*(2), 143–162. doi:10.1080/1554480X.2013.769196

Reinhardt, J. (2012). Accommodating divergent frameworks in analysis of technology-mediated L2 interaction. In M. Dooly, & R. O'Dowd (Eds.), *Researching online foreign language interaction and exchange* (pp. 45–77). Bern: Peter Lang.

Risager, K. (2005). Languaculture as a key concept in language and culture teaching. In B. Preisler, A. Fabricius, H. Haberland, S. Kjaerbeck, & K. Risager (Eds.), *The consequences of mobility* (pp. 185–196). Roskilde: Roskilde University, Department of Language and Culture.

Schmidt, R. (1990). The role of consciousness in second language learning. *Applied Linguistics, 11*, 129–158. doi:10.1093/applin/11.2.129

Schneider, & von der Emde, S. (2006). Conflicts in cyberspace: From communication breakdown to intercultural dialogue in online collaborations. In J. A. Belz, & S. L. Thorne (Eds.), *Internet-mediated intercultural foreign language education* (pp. 178–206). Boston, MA: Heinle & Heinle.

Smith, B. (2008). Methodological hurdles in capturing CMC data: The case of the missing self-repair. *Language Learning & Technology, 12*(1), 85–103.

Thorne, S. L. (2003). Artifacts and cultures-of-use in intercultural communication. *Language Learning & Technology, 7*(2), 38–67.

Tudini, V. (2003). Using native speakers in chat. *Language Learning & Technology, 7*(3), 141–159.

van Lier, L. (2004). *The ecology and semiotics of language learning: A sociocultural perspective*. Boston, MA: Dordrecht, Kluwer Academic.

Ware, P. (2005). "Missed" communication in online communication: Tensions in a German-American telecollaboration. *Language Learning & Technology, 9*(2), 64–89.

Ware, P., & Kramsch, C. (2005). Toward an intercultural stance: Teaching German and English through telecollaboration. *The Modern Language Journal, 89*(2), 190–205. doi:10.1111/j.1540-4781.2005.00274.x

Ware, P., & Rivas, B. (2012). Researching classroom integration of online language learning projects: Mixed methods approaches. In M. Dooly, & R. O'Dowd (Eds.), *Researching online foreign language interaction and exchange* (pp. 107–131). Bern: Peter Lang.

Warschauer, M. (Ed.). (1996a). *Telecollaboration in foreign language learning*. Honolulu, HI: Second Language Teaching & Curriculum Center, University of Hawai'i.

Warschauer, M. (1996b). Comparing face-to-face and electronic discussion in the second language classroom. *CALICO Journal, 13*(2), 7–26.

Whorf, B. L. (1956). *Language, thought, and reality: Selected writings of Benjamin Lee Whorf*, J. B. Carroll (Ed.). New York, NY: Wiley.

Appendix A. Sample word associations and sentence completions in *Cultura*

(http://cultura.mit.edu/1997-fall-mit-supaero-toulouse/)

1997 Fall – MIT/SUPAERO

Questionnaire type: Word Associations

- neighbors / voisins – Discussion
- responsibility / responsabilité - Discussion
- hierarchy / hiérarchie - Discussion
- government / gouvernement - Discussion
- store owner / commerçant - Discussion
- authority / autorité - Discussion
- youth / jeunesse - Discussion
- tradition / tradition - Discussion
- freedom / liberté - Discussion
- money / argent - Discussion
- vacation / vacances - Discussion
- civil servant / fonctionnaire - Discussion
- work / travail - Discussion
- France / France - Discussion
- United States / Etats-Unis - Discussion
- family / famille – Discussion
- grand-parents / grands-parents - Discussion
- elite / élite - Discussion
- politics / politique - Discussion
- suburbs / banlieue - Discussion

Questionnaire type: Sentence Completions

- A "good" neighbor is ... / Un "bon" voisin est ... - Discussion
- A "well-behaved" child is a ... / Un enfant "bien ... - Discussion
- A "good" doctor is a ... / Un "bon" médecin est ... - Discussion
- A "good" job is a ... / Un "bon" job est un ... - Discussion
- A "good" parent is ... / Un "bon" parent est un ... - Discussion
- A "good" teacher is a ... / Un "bon" prof est un ... - Discussion
- A "good" boss is a ... / Un "bon" patron est ... - Discussion
- A "good" friend is ... / Un "bon" ami est ... - Discussion
- A "successful" evening with friends ... / Une soirée "réussie" ... - Discussion
- A "polite" person is ... / Une personne "polie" est une ... - Discussion

An emic lens into online learning environments in PBL in undergraduate dentistry

Susan Bridges

Centre for the Enhancement of Teaching and Learning/Faculty of Education, The University of Hong Kong, Hong Kong, China

> Whilst face-to-face tutorial group interaction has been the focus of quantitative and qualitative studies in problem-based learning (PBL), little work has explored the independent learning phase of the PBL cycle from an interactionist perspective. An interactional ethnographic logic of inquiry guided collection and analysis of video recordings and learning artefacts across tied cycles of activity (multiple days and times) to identify evidence of learning in an undergraduate health sciences curriculum. An additional stimulated recall interview provided further emic perspectives of online learning during a self-directed learning session within the PBL cycle of activity. This approach guided the identification of key events, intertextual ties across chains of events, and the transcribing and mapping of changes in problem-solving across events, actors and times. Records included problem-based sessions in dental education, overtime video records, transcriptions, and analysis of online work and reflections on accounts constructed by undergraduate dental students. Key findings examined the role of online resources in supporting PBL curriculum design as well as provided "emic" insights into student knowledge-building processes. Interactionist analyses enabled the unfolding, recursive and re-iterative nature of disciplinary knowledge and identity construction across time and contexts through the use of more contextualized forms of representation as "evidence".

Introduction

The purpose of this paper is to explore how online resources, particularly digital learning objects, support independent study in a problem-based learning (PBL) curriculum in the Hong Kong health sciences education research context. Specifically, it examines how qualitative research in cross-disciplinary educational research can investigate the emic and etic (Lett, 1996) of undergraduate learning in dentistry by researching questions about the visible and invisible "how" of student engagement across physical (face-to-face) and virtual learning environments. Two of Hoadley's (2007) goals of e-learning research are relevant to this study: (a) producing theories that explain phenomena with e-learning; and (b) producing design models that permit construction of improved e-learning interventions. This small-scale, qualitative study, therefore, took up the opportunity to examine e-learning in a situated context in order to provide some explanatory insights into the phenomenon at hand. Insights from the research agenda within which this study was situated have led to major enhancements to curriculum design incorporating educational technologies in PBL, including adoption of a blended approach to the thoughtful inclusion of educational technologies to both the face-to-face and self-directed components of a PBL curriculum.

These initiatives resulted in a 2012 university-level "Outstanding Teaching Award (Team)". Early interactional ethnographic (IE) work examining portable interactive whiteboards (Bridges, Botelho, & Tsang, 2010) led to the full installation of interactive whiteboards linked to short-throw data projectors and laptops in each of the dedicated PBL rooms in two faculties. Work on trialling digital tools to support concept mapping within the PBL process (Bridges, Dyson, & Corbet, 2009) led to full implementation of the CMapTools™ (Institute for Human and Machine Cognition, www.ihmc.us) software into the learning management system (LMS). The theory and rationale behind concept mapping as well as their design and the use of the concept mapping software were then incorporated into the first-year experience in undergraduate dentistry. Further, the inclusion of 3-D digital learning objects into the LMS has been used to enhance PBL and case-based learning (Yang, Zhang, & Bridges, 2012). Ongoing interest in PBL and technology in health-sciences curricula in Hong Kong has also led to innovative implementations such as the use of synchronous web-conferencing in speech and hearing sciences (Ng, Bridges, Law, & Whitehill, 2014). As Vasiliou, Ioannou, Arh, Zaphiris, and Klobučar (2013) recently indicated, "technology enhanced and multimedia enriched problem-based learning (PBL) … is on the leading edge of PBL practice as technology is becoming an important tool for communication, collaboration, information retrieval, and knowledge creation" (p. 7). Research in the area, however, remains limited.

Background

PBL as pedagogic approach and curriculum design

PBL is an approach to learning that fosters collaboration and learner engagement in complex reasoning processes (Barrows & Tamblyn, 1980; Koh, Khoo, Wong, & Koh, 2008) to frame the acquisition of knowledge through understanding the dimensions of applied, ill-structured problems (Barrows, 1986; Butler, Inman, & Lobb, 2005; Savery, 2006). As such, historically, PBL is more closely aligned to small-group Socratic methods than to the lecture-based, post-industrial pedagogies of higher education in the more recent century. Meta analyses (Dochy, Segers, Van den Bossche, & Gijbels, 2003; Walker & Leary, 2009) and syntheses of meta-analyses (Prosser & Sze, 2014; Strobel & van Barneveld, 2009) indicate the positive effects of PBL on student learning. The characteristics of successful PBL have been found to be with regards to integration of disciplinary content; collaboration and teamwork; deep learning in the areas of application and synthesis of new knowledge; reflection; engagement with "real-world" problems and issues; and assessment processes which measure these facets (Lu, Bridges, & Hmelo-Silver, 2014). Prosser and Sze's (2014) review of meta-analyses and input–output studies in PBL documented benefits in terms of long-term retention of course content, short-term retention involving elaboration of new information, and the application of clinical skills and reasoning. Attainment of these characteristics of PBL is optimally achieved at both the curriculum design level from careful structuring and mapping of disciplinary content within and across years and at the classroom level through complex, problem-stimulated learning interactions facilitated in small, student-directed groups.

Process-oriented research has gained a clear understanding of how learning occurs within PBL tutorials (Hmelo-Silver, 2004; Schmidt, 1989; Yew, Chng, & Schmidt, 2011); however, it remains unclear as how in situ learning occurs during the independent inquiry phase between face-to-face classroom tutorials, referred to in PBL curricula as "self-directed learning" (SDL). Additionally obscure is our understanding of how students engage with educational technologies be it the multimodal resources provided via LMS or those accessed via open sources. This small-scale ethnographic study aims to explore two "black boxes" in PBL – SDL and the influence of educational technologies on the PBL learning process. In doing so, this study takes an emic approach to explore self-study practices among senior students. Specifically, this study addresses the question: *How are educational technologies consequential to student learning within and across the PBL cycle?*

Context: the PBL model used

The philosophy and structure of the 5-year PBL curriculum in this telling case of first-year undergraduate dentistry followed classic models premised on the use of complex, ill-defined, hypothetical problems grounded in real-life contexts to stimulate small group learning with an emphasis on active student engagement (Barrows, 1986, 1988). The curriculum was originally conceived to follow these premises (McGrath, Comfort, Luo, Samaranayake, & Clark, 2006) and has been reported as one of only three curricula worldwide as fitting the closest description of "pure" PBL curriculum in dental education (Winning & Townsend, 2007), with evaluations reflecting its impact on graduate outcomes (Yiu et al., 2011, 2012) and refinements to the final year experience supporting the curriculum's enquiry-based philosophy (Botelho, Lo, Bridges, McGrath, & Yiu, 2013). and has been reported as one of only three curricula worldwide as fitting the closest description of "pure" PBL curriculum in dental education (Winning & Townsend, 2007). As such, the PBL problems support vertical and horizontal integration of content across the curriculum (Barrows, 1986). An illustration of the tutorial process as enacted at the time of data collection (2009) is illustrated in Figure 1.

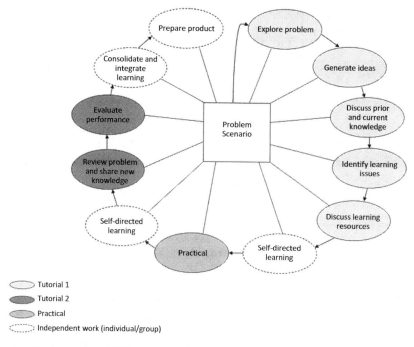

Figure 1. Problem cycle (2009) as adopted in the study (see also Bridges, Green, Botelho, & Tsang, 2014).

This approach closely mirrored the "closed-loop" or reiterative problem design (Barrows, 1986) in which (a) the problem comes first, followed by (b) collaborative knowledge-building in tutorials followed by (c) a period of dedicated SDL and then closing with (d) a second tutorial for consolidation, synthesis and application of research to coming to a fuller understanding of the problem at hand. Barrows (1986) originally argued that such a closed-loop design achieves the highest attainment of all four key PBL educational objectives of

- structuring of knowledge for use in clinical contexts;
- developing an effective clinical reasoning process;
- developing effective self-directed learning skills; and
- increasing motivation for learning. (pp. 481–482)

These founding principles have been supported more recently in a review of PBL research (Walker & Leary, 2009).

Educational technologies introduced to support this closed-loop model included an LMS (WebCT™) via which the problem statement and supporting materials were simultaneously released to all tutorial groups in the same year of the dental undergraduate programme at the beginning of the first tutorial (see Figure 1). Supporting materials in the telling case for this study included images related to the oral condition, such as a clinical radiograph, a study cast (model made from the patient's mouth), and a photograph of the oral condition specific to the disease under discussion. As such, these provided a rich multimodal array of materials to support student-led inquiry into the problem case at hand. At the time of the case under analysis, students used an electric printboard to provide a printout of the group's notes generated during the first tutorial including the "facts" (identified from the problem statement), "ideas" (hypotheses as to what biomedical, psychosocial, etc., factors are at play) and "learning issues" (topics for research and preparation for the second tutorial). This printout was routinely used to assist research during the ensuing SDL phase and as a reference during the final tutorial as the group brought the case to a close. The closed-loop design supported by the LMS, therefore, enabled the inclusion of digital texts for rich, multimodal stimuli and resources for student learning.

Research design

Materials and methods

Ethical approval was gained and records were collected from problem-based sessions across one problem cycle (2 weeks, February 2009) for one PBL group ($n = 8$) in their 4th year of a 5-year Bachelor of Dental Surgery (BDS) curriculum. The selection of the problem scenario and year level for this paper was due to both the richness of the variety of modalities in the problem case's design and the high degree of familiarity with PBL of these more senior students. Session types recorded across the problem cycle (see Figure 1) included whole-group face-to-face tutorials and one member's initial self-directed session of online research immediately following the PBL tutorial. The collection of recordings over time included videos of in-class tutorial learning, Camtasia™ screen capture recordings of self-directed online work, and a video and screen capture of a stimulated recall interview session. The stimulated recall interview was conducted with the student (S) controlling the playback of the screen recording from the initial SDL conducted in the computer laboratory. The interviewer (I) then provided prompts to further elicit thought processes whilst conducting online searching. All recordings were transcribed using Transana™.

An IE logic of inquiry (Castanheira, Crawford, Dixon, & Green, 2000; Putney, Green, Dixon, Duran, & Yeager, 2000) guided collection and analysis of video recordings and learning artefacts across tied cycles of PBL activity (multiple days and times) to identify evidence of learning in addressing the key research question. This approach guided the identification of key events, intertextual ties across chains of events, transcribing and mapping changes in problem-solving across events, actors and times in this health sciences curriculum (Bridges, Botelho, Green, & Chau, 2012; Bridges et al., 2014). The IE approach provided a clear organizational framework for the artefacts collected across the study. Records included overtime video recordings in dental education of one 4th year group's problem-based tutorials, a volunteer's post-tutorial engagement with online resources and a stimulated recall interview of the self-learning session. Transcriptions of the latter were seen as reflective accounts constructed by one dental student.

Tracing of key events of a "telling case" (Mitchell, 1984) of this one student's engagement with the problem process provided a principled approach to gaining emic understandings of learner engagement with the problem process. Analysis of phases of on-screen activity via Camtasia™ screen capture recordings and the reflective discourse surrounding the playback of this recorded on-screen activity in the stimulated recall interview supported emic insights both from the perspective of curriculum developer researcher and student reflector into how online activity was both stimulated and produced by the PBL process.

Analysis

Figure 2 provides an event map of the major transitions recorded within the PBL group's tutorial discussions (video recordings) and during one student's initial SDL (Camtasia™ screen capture and interview video recordings) in the week between face-to-face tutorials.

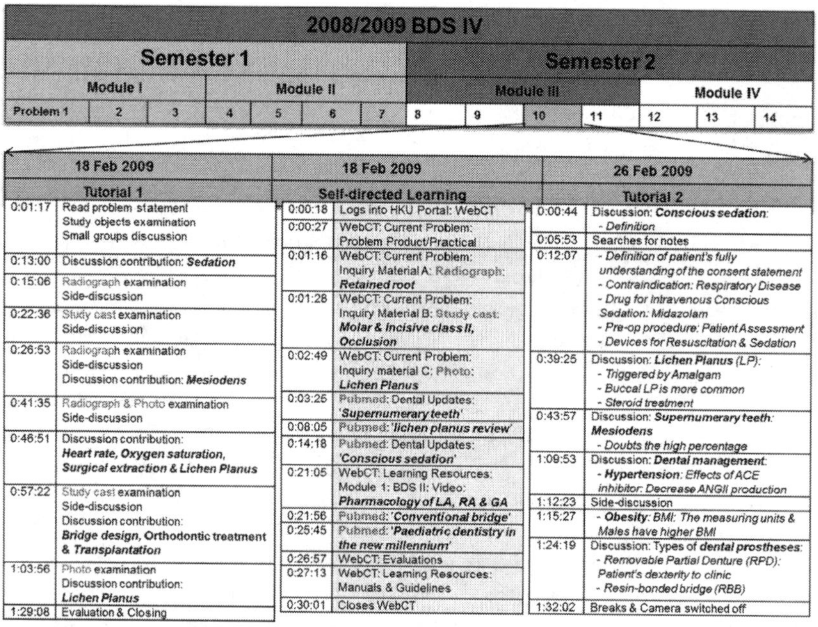

Figure 2. Event map of major transitions in a PBL cycle.

The event map does not indicate non-recorded events in the PBL cycle such as the practical session (usually a hands-on workshop) and the remaining SDL sessions which occurred across the 2-week cycle; however, it provides a window into the evolving discursive activity of the two tutorials and the first stage of SDL undertaken immediately following the first tutorial.

The event map (Figure 2) is anchored to one 4th year student PBL experience across one problem cycle both with his group in the tutorials and individually in his SDL. Tutorial 1 (18 February 2009) in column 1 is listed as phases according to activity transitions, particularly those stimulated by the multimodal inquiry materials (radiograph, study cast, photo) provided within the problem materials as a further stimulus to student inquiry. As per the problem cycle (Figure 1), students identified the "facts" evident in the problem scenario and arising from the inquiry materials. They then hypothesized by brainstorming their "ideas" and identifying prior knowledge. Finally, they established the gaps in their current understanding and identified the "learning issues" to be researched and the possible sources of information.

The single recorded SDL session (18 February 2009) in column 2 indicates the various transition moves the volunteer 4th year group member (S) made between resources accessed via educational technologies. These included resources provided by the curriculum designers via the dedicated LMS used at the time (WebCT™) and open-source materials accessed by the student during online searching, in this case an online medical database (PubMed).

Tutorial 2 (26 February 2009) in column 3 illustrates the topical shifts in the class discussion as the group shared their research on the "learning issues" or topics identified for research – supernumerary (additional) teeth, lichen planus (a type of skin disease), hypertension (high blood pressure) and obesity, conscious sedation, dental prostheses. After sharing new knowledge arising from independent research, the group then worked to collaboratively evaluate and synthesize new information in the light of the problem at hand.

Of particular note to the consequential nature of learning in PBL was the significant role of educational materials and visual resources in the first two phases (tutorial 1 and SDL) in informing the discussion held in the final phase (tutorial 2).

SDL is usually conducted individually or in smaller groups and is a research phase wherein students search for information regarding the designated learning topics (learning issues) agreed upon in the tutorial. The screen capture recording of computer-based activity in the initial self-directed phase clearly ties topically and visually with the prior resources and discussion in tutorial 1; however, it remains unclear as to how the student saw these resources as consequential to the knowledge construction process across the various phases of the problem cycle which is central to PBL. A further stimulated recall interview then provided emic insights into the knowledge-building processes in problem-based inquiry.

The stimulated interview data utilized a think-aloud protocol whereby one 4th year undergraduate dental student's screen capture of his own learning activity during one self-directed study session in the computer laboratory immediately following tutorial 1 was used as the stimulus for an open-ended interview. Each of the excerpts below indicates one student's (S) reflection which has been prompted by the recording of personal on-screen learning activity and the prompt questions posed by the interviewer (I). All activity is describing the student's initial searching during SDL immediately after the first tutorial.

S's initial online activity was to log-in to the LMS (0:00:18) to review the assignment task referred to as a "product" (00:00:27) to confirm the venue and topic of the upcoming

INTERDISCIPLINARY AND INTERCULTURAL PROGRAMMES

Excerpt 1.   (0:01:16) Radiograph.

S: Mmm… sure. Ah… Because we've mentioned something about ah… the bridges and the dental condition of the ah… the missing teeth and the retained root.
I: Mmm
S: So I need to take a look maybe… after… after a lesson and just thinking. And also I have our "Idea Sheet" printed out and so I can refer back to where is the retained root and their condition about it.

"practical" – a hands-on workshop linked to one of the learning issues set for the current problem. He then navigated to the "Current Problem" to review the various multimodal inquiry materials, including clinical images such as a photograph and radiograph. His justification for viewing the radiograph is evident in Excerpt 1 where he expressed a desire to re-confirm a face-to-face discussion topic regarding "retained root".

An intervisual link (Kress, 2000) is formed between this activity and the classroom artefact, in this case an "Idea Sheet" printout, which he has brought to the SDL session in the computer laboratory. The student's ensuing online activity moves to a faculty-provided digital learning object in the form of a Quick Time Virtual Reality (QTVR) study model generated from the solid object provided within classes (see Excerpt 2). As Kress (2000) noted

> Technologies of information lend themselves to "visualisation", the phenomenon in which information initially stored in written form is "translated" into visual form, largely because the transport of information is seen as more efficient in the visual rather than the verbal mode. (p. 183)

For students enrolled in dental surgery, the haptic "feel" of a study model in tandem with the visual analysis of the shape of the dentition (arrangement of teeth) is important to

Excerpt 2.   (0:01:28) Study cast.

S: Ah… and also ah… I am taking a look about ah… same for taking… looking at the study cast.
I: Mmm
S: Also finding out ah any information that I missed during the PBL lessons
I: Mmm. So can you go back a bit and really talk us through the study cast, so what were you actually… you spent a little bit time with it, so step by step, what were you thinking about when you were looking at the study cast?
S: Ah… first… after… ah… when opening about this study cast
I: Mm
S: I need to figure how to… how to… how to ah take control because it's the first time that this study cast is uploaded.
I: OK.
S: Yeah… so I try to rotate it around and keep using it like that.
I: OK, so you're just getting used to the tool.
S: Yes, yeah, so after ah… knowing ah… how to use it and then I start looking at ah some ah dental information, like the overjet, as I've shown it here, and also the molar class and the incisive class. Because one of the learning issues is the ah… incisive class two
I: Mm
S: So I take a look on how ah… how the patient presents with it. Yeah and also later I found out that ah… at a certain rotation angle it can be ah… overlapped. You can take a look on the occlusion.

INTERDISCIPLINARY AND INTERCULTURAL PROGRAMMES

Excerpt 3.   (0:03:25) PubMed searching.

S: After looking at all these information then I start ah looking at resources.
I: Mm Mm
S: Yeah. Usually I look… find some journals in the *PubMed*
I: Mm Mm
S: Yeah, and ah… apart from reading journals, I usually I'll take a look at the textbooks, some medical textbooks which we already have at home. So ah… when using a computer I'd like to find some more updated information because something on the textbook may not be too updated.
I: Yup
S: So I start ah find a journals, first start with a basic, like ah… typing some keywords, for example like "lichen planus" or "supernumerary teeth". Ah… first search about it, and then later…
I: Now why "supernumerary teeth"?
S: Yeah, and then ah… when taking a look on first a few journals it's mostly about the ah… the research so I add the "review" [search term]. Yeah, to find some basic information before studying in depth.
I: and supernumery teeth was a learning issue?
S: Yes, it's one of the learning issues. Yeah and so I ….find the ah… the full text in *Dental Update*.

---

diagnosing the case. In supporting clinical diagnosis, the inclusion of a visualization of the type of malocclusion (poor alignment of upper and lower teeth) described in the print case, both as solid and virtual objects, enabled student analysis.

This student's mouse manipulation of the 3-D study cast is initially driven by his psychomotor need to control how the mouse influences directionality of the object – *I try to rotate it around*. Upon achieving a satisfactory level of mastery with the QTVR tool, the student moves again to highly strategic analysis driven by the discussions in tutorial 1 and the learning issues the group has identified:

> I start looking at ah some ah dental information, like the overjet, as I've shown it here, and also the molar class and the incisive class. Because one of the learning issues is the ah… incisive class two.

A key transition then occurs as the student moves from confirming the outcome of the group discussion from the online resources provided by curriculum planners via the LMS to independent searching for information as described in Excerpt 3.

Excerpt 3 reflects the strategies this student employs in this initial stage of independent learning in moving from hardcopy textbooks to finding more "updated information". Given the overwhelming amount of online information, this student then strategically includes the term "review" in the search strategy. This is significant to an issue students also experience in adjusting to the relatively open nature of a PBL curriculum, especially in determining the breadth and depth of information sought. Demonstrated in Excerpt 3 is the student's strategy to reduce both the volume and complexity of the articles found as a result of online searching. Inclusion of the term "review" limits the papers to those giving a broad but principled account of the field regarding the specific learning issue at hand (i.e. "supernumerary teeth") that goes beyond a simple encyclopaedic search with a platform such as Wikipedia. However, it does not take an undergraduate student into literature beyond their level such as that expected for doctoral students and researchers. The student's ensuing reflection on search practices in Excerpt 4 provides further emic insights into this student's process of information management.

INTERDISCIPLINARY AND INTERCULTURAL PROGRAMMES

Excerpt 4:   Cascade searching.

I: So you are back to the *PubMed* results…
S: After ah… usually taking a look of one of the journals and at the right hand side there's some related articles, that's why i'd take a look on the titles whether it is related or not. Yeah.

....

S: Yep, and that's this one. And after taking a look on ah.. these journal, and I save it down as well. And then I … take a look on the others related articles and see whether ah… others are related or not.
I: OK
S: And these are some of the related articles and as I mentioned before there is also the review articles, yeah. Review articles, yeah. Ah.. and then ah.. after seeing those related articles and I ah.. again look at the search result again.
I: OK back in *PubMed*
S: Yeah… and see whether there are still other related articles. Then usually I will search about ah… look at the hr… may be.. ah… the top 30 related articles because I found that at most ah… after 30 most of them are not related. Yep.
I: OK, thirty, three zero
S: Yep, three zero. Yep, and I think that's the 4th one
I: OK, there you're going…
S: And this about the histological consideration. And then after that I start search about the ah.. the "sedation". It's again another learning issue.
I: Hmm. Does in this one the sedation in both exist in that problem?
S: Ah yes… mainly about different types of sedation, inhalation, sedation, oral sedation and also the IV sedation. Yeah. And because ah… most of the ah…sedation is very common in paediatric history, so I start ah… searching some keywords in paediatric dentistry and also ah… sedation like that. And finally I come out with ah… the one of these journals.

…

S: And after that ah .. I have ah… continue searching about ah from the dental update.. in the keyword
I: Right, "conscious sedation"
S: Yeah, and then take a look on the full abstract. That's from the *Dental Update* so I decided to copy the whole ah.. the headings into it and copy and paste it. And you can find ah…the one two three and four…
I: Right, you're still chasing the series, yep.
S: And that's the third one, and which is the most related, the "inhalation sedation" but others… I have ah…although this is not related to the full series.

Excerpt 4 illuminates the type of knowledge-seeking activity this particular student engages in. The student not only searches for the key terms of the specified learning issues and limits this with "review" but also, from experience, has determined how many abstracts to screen/skim ($n = 30$) for selection of full articles. This highly strategic triage process has enabled this student, in approximately 26 minutes, to navigate from

- (a) confirming his goals and learning targets for this session (Excerpt 1) to
- (b) reviewing a 3-D digital learning object as an inquiry material to (Excerpt 2) to
- (c) conducting a strategic database search (Excerpts 3 and 4) to
- (d) finally expanding his search to examine related links to the articles yielded from the online search.

This type of "cascade" searching with each stage building logically from the previous one provides an important scaffold to manage the, at times, daunting flow of medical information now available at students' fingertips. Indeed, this highly stratified and organized approach to the use of both faculty provided and open access online resources emphasizes the issue of autonomy and scaffolding in digital PBL which has been noted in primary schooling (Van Loon, Ros, & Martens, 2012). It indicates that an undergraduate health sciences student who is well-versed in PBL becomes a highly strategic user of online information deftly weaving between that which has been provided as in-house research on a dedicated learning management platform and online information. As such, the advanced PBL learner is not only able to work autonomously in their SDL time but also to impose a scaffolded structure to their online inquiry which supports learning within and across the larger PBL problem cycle.

Discussion

This study has sought to provide emic insights into PBL by addressing the key research question: *How are educational technologies consequential to student learning within and across the PBL cycle?* By adopting an IE framework combined with a think-aloud protocol, the researcher is able to not only identify and trace consequential learning across a problem cycle but is also able to gain further emic insights into a student's online learning practices and how these support autonomous learning in PBL. In making student learning practices and processes visible through the research design, two areas of particular conceptual interest have become evident in this study. First, the IE approach provided methodological tools and perspectives to describe, map and triangulate observations, which led to insights into how students work with agility in seeking relevant information and developing "flexible knowledge". A second conceptual consideration arising from this ethnography is the role of intervisual links in supporting multimodal learning in an inquiry-based pedagogic approach.

Flexible knowledge

The notion of "flexible knowledge" challenges transmissive pedagogic approaches (Hmelo-Silver, 2004). Rather than being a static "gift" from the teacher, knowledge becomes a fluid dynamic facilitated by both tutor and peers. Zygmut Baumann's (2000) notion of fluid modernity aligns philosophically with this notion of dynamism: as the pace of change has escalated in knowledge economies, so too has the way we access and perceive information. This is effectively indicated by patterns of sociolinguistic change. For example, the term "googling" has evolved linguistically from a brand name and noun to a verb whose meaning implies searching for an answer online. In a world of fluid modernity, information is no longer restricted to the professions or the privileged. For learners, the implications are that what one needs to know has shifted from finding the best reference text to searching for the best online resource (be it website, journal article or e-book). New skills in online searching begin to define the new learner. Skills such as efficiency and efficacy in devising and applying online search strategies begin to differentiate the successful learner/searcher from the time waster who has become lost in the morass of online information. In the case above, student S's use of faculty-provided resources and the application of self-acquired online searching behaviours saw a move from low-level information seeking to engagement with higher order cognition such as synthesis and evaluation of a variety of information to the application of new knowledge towards resolution of the puzzle at hand.

What was made evident in the recall interview was the understanding of the learner of PBL as a pedagogic approach. Samuelowicz and Bain's (2001) study of academics across both teacher-and-learner-centred curricula indicated a tension between the different conceptions of knowledge inherent to the pedagogic approach. Evident in the case above was the student's clarity with regards to the role of SDL and, indeed, the inquiry-based approach of PBL itself. The student appropriated the requisite roles and strategies of a PBL learner by taking control of the learning process. This was conveyed in his interview account of his online actions through his clarity in the role of searching within the collaborative, student-centred process. His independent studies were a direct result of artefacts and discursive constructions within the first tutorial and the online resources he accessed in his independent searching for information. At the close of the online session, the student shared the articles yielded from the online search with his PBL group via email. This final distribution of resources with the collective learning community at the end of his initial information-gathering session also reflects his understanding of his role in the collaborative knowledge-building process that is PBL.

Intervisuality and talked images

Like Kress's (2000, 2010) exploration of the role of the visual image in making cognitive connections across multiple images in embedded contexts, Freitas and Castanheira (2007) argued for the contextualized nature of image use, seeing the role of "visual representation to convey meaning and support conceptual understanding of disciplinary and scientific concepts" (p. 151). Their study of visual images in high school biology indicated that the "meanings of an image are convened through a simultaneous use of various semiotic means in teaching processes" including the image itself, the talk generated over time and the gestural supports a speaker uses to explicate the image and their interpretation (p. 161). These findings are supported by IE analysis in undergraduate dental education (Bridges, Botelho, et al., 2012; Bridges et al., 2014) where visual representations were both receptive stimuli for and productive syntheses produced through blended learning.

The current study held a specific focus in more closely examining what occurs intervisually in the knowledge construction process when the student is in an independent phase of learning outside the face-to-face, facilitated, collaborative PBL context of the tutorial room. What was evident in this study was that the 4th year dental student exhibited how adeptly he was able to interweave between various semiotic images to build conceptual understanding of the problem to be addressed. This student's initial navigation during SDL provided a strategic re-orientation to the images supplied and discussed in class which resulted in reminding, focusing and looking for anything the group discussion may have missed. The student's alacrity in identifying the intervisual links between the PBL stimulus images and online 3-D models and the issues identified by the group on the printout quickly established a referential tie between the online support materials and the in-class images and solid models.

Methodological considerations

Early progenitors in the PBL literature (Barrows, 1988; Schmidt, 1989) and the ensuing generation of PBL scholars (Hmelo-Silver & Barrows, 2008; Lu et al., 2014; Yew et al., 2011) indicate the strength of the social constructivist (Palincsar, 1998) design of the PBL cycle in supporting knowledge-building. In the telling case above, the application of an IE approach, coupled with an introspective, think-aloud protocol in the form of a stimulated recall interview, provided greater transparency as to how knowledge-building was achieved by one student within and across a problem cycle. The dual approach allowed not only a principled mapping of the enacted curriculum but also allowed the unveiling of layers of the experienced curriculum hitherto not visible.

Utilizing this research design, emic features of the learning process, such as student activity during independent, SDL when supported with online materials provided via an LMS were laid visible to analysis. The stimulated recall interview using ethnographic artefacts in the form of screen capture prompted not only learner introspection and metacognitive reflective analysis but also brought to light the student's ways of working with information and texts within the process of active knowledge construction. The process of making visible the interaction between micro-level student learning processes and macro-level curriculum design principles provided practical insights, which then supported the process of curriculum renewal and transformation towards what was locally conceived as "PBL2.0" (Bridges et al., 2010).

Conclusions

This small-scale IE study has, to some degree, addressed areas of need in higher education research. Specifically, it begins to address some of the gaps in the higher education research literature identified by Savin-Baden, McFarlane, and Savin-Baden's (2008) review, including

- "There is a need to develop commonly-understood discourses about teaching and learning, as a prerequisite to being able to make teaching and learning regimes explicit and challenging them openly.
- There needs to be further exploration into the impact of diverse teaching methods on the students' experience.
- There is a need for further studies into conceptions of interactivity and related practices.
- e-Learning pedagogy is largely missing from the literature and needs to be developed and researched.
- The practices and pedagogy associated with inquiry-based forms of learning continue to be troublesome, and require further research.
- Research into learning spaces (that reaches beyond that of design for learning) requires further study." (pp. 7–9)

In making teaching and learning regimes explicit, work in health sciences education has begun to examine the impact of educational technologies on PBL, addressing the "troublesome" issue of the practices and pedagogy of this inquiry-based form. Alkhasawneh et al.'s (2008) study of PBL in nurse education found that students had a higher multimodal preference after experiencing a modality-rich PBL environment (models, demonstrations, discussions, debates, Q&A and role-playing). Indeed in considering the role of digital learning materials in PBL as one example of the diverse pedagogies promoting interactivity, an experimental study in ophthalmology found the value-added benefit of digital PBL cases to be in terms of stimulating student interest and motivating them to "further improve diagnosis and problem-handling skills" (Kong, Li, Wang, Sun, & Zhang, 2009). While previous ethnographic studies have drawn upon video analysis to establish discursive "storylines" in scientific inquiry (McDonald & Kelly, 2007), little ethnographic work has examined the trajectory of scientific inquiry beyond the classroom. When considering the PBL cycle (Lu et al., 2014), little research has been undertaken to explore out-of-class learning during designated, independent, SDL episodes and the consequential nature of this phase to the face-to-face facilitated tutorials (Bridges, Botelho, et al., 2012; Bridges et al., 2014). The IE approach adopted, therefore, framed the identification of key events, intertextual ties across chains of events, the transcribing and mapping of changes in problem-solving across events, actors and times.

In understanding the phenomenon of learning with digital resources, the collection of a range of emic and etic data enabled analysis of in-class tutorial discussion and post-class online self-study. Adoption of an IE approach provided a principled method for data collection and analysis that, when combined with stimulated recall methodology, further enabled the uncovering of "emic" knowledge-building processes within PBL that had not been previously visible. Analysis of the unfolding, recursive and reiterative nature of multimodal texts across learning environments established a new body of "evidence," which indicated how group learning in tutorial discussions of real learning objects was reinforced individually in SDL when virtual representations of the same objects were provided as self-study resource. Explanatory theories assisted understanding of how 4th year dental education students accessed a range of educational technologies to support learning within and across a problem cycle, including SDL. Analysis supports learning theories of the role of visual representations in learning and the building of flexible knowledge. This study, therefore, has made visible how the accessing of digital representations of PBL stimulus materials between tutorials supports student learning in a problem-based curriculum in an English-medium dental curriculum.

Ongoing research is adopting the IE framework to explore the nuances of technology-enabled PBL across three health sciences curricula (dentistry, medicine, and speech and hearing sciences). Opportunities exist to further explore the impact of such research across multiple learning contexts (clinical, simulated, etc.) in PBL health sciences curricula. Implications for further studies in other professional higher education contexts such as teacher education, engineering, law and architecture are also evident, and these would be promising sites for further exploration of the issues indicated in this small-scale study.

Acknowledgement

This research was conducted with technical support of Ms Jessica Wong, and her assistance is greatly appreciated.

Funding

The University of Hong Kong Seed Fund for Basic Research.

References

Alkhasawneh, I. M., Mrayyan, M. T., Docherty, C., Alashram, S., & Yousef, H. Y. (2008). Problem-based learning (PBL): Assessing students' learning preferences using vark. *Nurse Education Today, 28*(5), 572–579. doi:10.1016/j.nedt.2007.09.012

Barrows, H. S. (1986). A taxonomy of problem-based learning-methods. *Medical Education, 20*(6), 481–486. doi:10.1111/j.1365-2923.1986.tb01386.x

Barrows, H. S. (1988). *The tutorial process*. Springfield: Southern Illinois University Press.

Barrows, H. S., & Tamblyn, R. (1980). *Problem-based learning: An approach to medical education*. New York, NY: Springer.

Baumann, Z. (2000). *Liquid modernity*. Cambridge: Polity Press.

Botelho, M. G., Lo, E. C. M., Bridges, S. M., McGrath, C. P. J., & Yiu, C. K. Y. (2013). Journal-based learning, a new learning experience building on PBL at HKU. *European Journal of Dental Education, 17*, e120–e125. doi:10.1111/j.1600-0579.2012.00771.x

Bridges, S. M., Botelho, M. G., Green, J., & Chau, A. C. M. (2012). Multimodality in PBL: An interactional ethnography. In S. Bridges, C. McGrath, & T. Whitehill (Eds.), *Researching problem-based learning in clinical education: The next generation* (pp. 99–120). Dordrecht: Springer.

Bridges, S. M., Botelho, M. G., & Tsang, C. S. P. (2010). PBL2.0: Blended learning for an interactive, problem-based pedagogy. *Medical Education, 11*(44), 1135.

Bridges, S. M., Dyson, J. E., & Corbet, E. F. (2009). Blended learning, knowledge co-construction and undergraduate group work. *Medical Education, 43*(5), 490–491. doi:10.1111/j.1365-2923.2009.03345.x

Bridges, S. M., Green, J., Botelho, M. G., & Tsang, P. C. S. (2014). Blended learning and PBL: An interactional ethnographic approach to understanding knowledge construction in-situ. In A. Walker, H. Leary, C. Hmelo-Silver, & P. A. Ertmer (Eds.), *Essential readings in problem-based learning*. Purdue, IN: Purdue Press.

Bridges, S. M., McGrath, C., & Whitehill, T. (2012). The next generation: Research directions in PBL. In S. M. Bridges, C. McGrath, & T. Whitehill (Eds.), *Researching problem-based learning in clinical education: The next generation* (pp. 225–232). Dordrecht: Springer.

Butler, R., Inman, D., & Lobb, D. (2005). Problem-based learning and the medical school: Another case of the emperor's new clothes? *Advances in Physiology Education, 29*(4), 194–196.

Castanheira, M. L., Crawford, T., Dixon, C. N., & Green, J. L. (2000). Interactional ethnography: An approach to studying the social construction of literate practices. *Linguistics and Education, 11*(4), 353–400. doi:10.1016/s0898-5898(00)00032-2

Collins, A. (2006). Cognitive apprenticeship. In R. K. Sawyer (Ed.), *Cambridge handbook of the learning sciences* (pp. 47–60). Cambridge: Cambridge University Press.

Dochy, F., Segers, M., Van den Bossche, P., & Gijbels, D. (2003). Effects of problem-based learning: A meta-analysis. *Learning and Instruction, 13*(5), 533–568. doi:10.1016/s0959-4752(02)00025-7

Freitas, C. A., & Castanheira, M. L. (2007). Talked images: Examining the contextualised nature of image use. *Pedagogies: An International Journal, 2*(3), 151–164. doi:10.1080/15544800701366456

Hmelo-Silver, C. E. (2004). Problem-based learning: What and how do students learn? *Educational Psychology Review, 16*(3), 235–266. doi:10.1023/B:EDPR.0000034022.16470.f3

Hmelo-Silver, C. E., & Barrows, H. S. (2008). Facilitating collaborative knowledge building. *Cognition and Instruction, 26*, 48–94. doi:10.1080/07370000701798495

Hoadley, C. (2007). Learning sciences theories and methods for E-learning researchers. In R. Andrews & C. Haythornthwaite (Ed.), *Sage handbook of e-learning research*. London: SAGE Publications. doi:10.4135/9781848607859

Koh, G. C.-H., Khoo, H. E., Wong, M. L., & Koh, D. (2008). The effects of problem-based learning during medical school on physician competency: A systematic review. *Canadian Medical Association Journal, 178*(1), 34–41. doi:10.1503/cmaj.070565

Kong, J., Li, X., Wang, Y., Sun, W., & Zhang, J. (2009). Effect of digital problem-based learning cases on student learning outcomes in ophthalmology courses. *Archives of Ophthalmology, 127*(9), 1211–1214. doi:10.1001/archophthalmol.2009.110

Kress, G. (2000). Multimodality. In B. Cope & M. Kalantzis (Eds.), *Multiliteracies* (pp. 182–202). London: Routledge.

Kress, G. (2010). *Multimodality: A social semiotic approach to contemporary communication*. London: Routledge.

Lett, J. (1996). Emic/etic distinctions. In D. Levinson & M. Ember (Eds.), *Encyclopedia of cultural anthropology* (pp. 382–383). New York, NY: Henry Holt and Company.

Lu, J., Bridges, S. M., & Hmelo-Silver, C. (2014). Problem-based learning. In R. K. Sawyer (Ed.), *Cambridge handbook of learning sciences* (2nd ed., pp. 298–318). New York, NY: Cambridge University Press.

McDonald, S., & Kelly, G. J. (2007). Understanding the construction of a science storyline in a chemistry classroom. *Pedagogies: An International Journal, 2*(3), 165–177. doi:10.1080/15544800701366563

McGrath, C., Comfort, M. B., Luo, Y., Samaranayake, L. P., & Clark, C. D. (2006). Application of an interactive computer program to manage a problem-based dental curriculum. *Journal of Dental Education, 70*(4), 387–397.

Mitchell, J. C. (1984). Typicality and the case study. In R. F. Ellen (Ed.), *Ethnographic research* (pp. 238–240). New York, NY: Academic Press.

Ng, M. L., Bridges, S., Law, S. P., & Whitehill, T. (2014). Designing, implementing and evaluating an online problem-based learning (PBL) environment-A pilot study. *Clinical Linguistics & Phonetics, 28*(1–2), 117–130. doi:10.3109/02699206.2013.807879

Palincsar, A. S. (1998). Social constructivist perspectives on teaching and learning. *Annual Review of Psychology, 49*, 345–375. doi:10.1146/annurev.psych.49.1.345

Prosser, M., & Sze, D. (2014). Problem-based learning: Student learning experiences and outcomes. *Clinical Linguistics and Phonetics, 28*(1–2), 131–142. doi:10.3109/02699206.2013.820351

Putney, L. G., Green, J. L., Dixon, C., Duran, R., & Yeager, B. (2000). Consequential progressions: Exploring collective-individual development in a bilingual classroom. In C. D. Lee & P. Smagorinsky (Eds.), *Vygotskian perspectives on literacy research: Constructing meaning through collaborative inquiry* (pp. 86–126). New York, NY: Cambridge University Press.

Samuelowicz, K., & Bain, J. D. (2001). Revisiting academics' beliefs about teaching and learning. *Higher Education, 41*(3), 299–325. doi:10.1023/A:1004130031247

Savery, J. R. (2006). Overview of problem-based learning: Definitions and distinctions. *Interdisciplinary Journal of Problem-Based Learning, 1*(3).

Savin-Baden, M., McFarlane, L., & Savin-Baden, J. (2008). *Influencing thinking and practices about teaching and learning in higher education: An interpretive meta-ethnography*. York: Higher Education Academy. Retrieved from https://www.heacademy.ac.uk/sites/default/files/InfluencingThinking.pdf

Schmidt, H. G. (1989). The rationale behind problem-based learning. In M. J. L. H. G. Schmidt, M. W. De Vries, & J. M. Greep (Ed.), *New directions for medical education* (pp. 105–111). New York, NY: Springer-Verlag.

Strobel, J., & van Barneveld, A. (2009). When is PBL more effective? A meta-synthesis of meta-analyses comparing PBL to conventional classrooms. *Interdisciplinary Journal of Problem-Based Learning, 3*(1), 44–58.

Townsend, G., & Winning, T. (2011). Research in PBL – Where to from here for dentistry? *European Journal of Dental Education, 15*(3), 193–198. doi:10.1111/j.1600-0579.2010.00655.x

Van Loon, A.-M., Ros, A., & Martens, R. (2012). Motivated learning with digital learning tasks: What about autonomy and structure? *Educational Technology Research and Development, 60*(6), 1015–1032. doi:10.1007/s11423-012-9267-0

Vasiliou, C., Ioannou, A., Arh, T., Zaphiris, P., & Klobučar, T., (2013). *Technology enhanced problem based learning*. Proceedings of 32nd international conference on Organizational Science Development, Portorož. Retrieved August 27, 2014, from http://infospaces.cyprusinteractionlab.com/wp-content/uploads/2013/03/Vasiliou-et-al.-Portoroz2013.pdf

Walker, A. E., & Leary, H. (2009). A problem based learning meta analysis: Differences across problem types, implementation types, disciplines, and assessment levels. *Interdisciplinary Journal of Problem-based Learning, 3*, 12–43.

Winning, T., & Townsend, G. (2007). Problem-based learning in dental education: What's the evidence for and against ... and is it worth the effort? *Australian Dental Journal, 52*(1), 2–9. doi:10.1111/j.1834-7819.2007.tb00458.x

Yang, Y., Zhang, L., & Bridges, S. (2012). Blended learning in dentistry: 3-D resources for inquiry-based learning. *Knowledge Management & E-Learning: An International Journal (KM&EL), 4*(2), 217–230.

Yew, E. H. J., Chng, E., & Schmidt, H. G. (2011). Is learning in problem-based learning cumulative? *Advances in Health Sciences Education, 16*(4), 449–464. doi:10.1007/s10459-010-9267-y

Yiu, C., McGrath, C., Bridges, S., Corbet, E., Botelho, M., Dyson, J., & Chan, L. K. (2011). Graduates' perceived preparedness for dental practice from PBL and traditional curriculum. *Journal of Dental Education, 75*(9), 1270–1279.

Yiu, C., McGrath, C., Bridges, S., Corbet, E., Botelho, M., Dyson, J., & Chan, L. K. (2012). Self-perceived preparedness for dental practice amongst graduates of The University of Hong Kong's integrated PBL dental curriculum. *European Journal of Dental Education, 16*(1), e96–e105. doi:10.1111/j.1600-0579.2011.00681.x

Designing interdisciplinary instruction: exploring disciplinary and conceptual differences as a resource

W. Douglas Baker and Elisabeth Däumer

Department of English Language and Literature, Eastern Michigan University, Ypsilanti, MI, USA

This article presents a "telling case" of an interdisciplinary, team-teaching experience that explores how participants eschewed *ethnocentricism* of their fields of study in order to learn from each other, while providing instruction to students and analysing data collected from the class (a graduate course on literature and pedagogy). Through the process, the participants (a professor of English education and a professor of literature) ground the perspectives of literary interpretation in their field of study and *languaculture*, and developed a conceptual framework that guided their interactions and analysis of the discursive actions of the class. An ethnographic perspective served as the conceptual frame and informed how the participants observed, described, and developed claims about classroom interactions. Through this study, the participants answer calls for more examples of how faculty in higher education engage in interdisciplinary teaching and research and the need for faculty to develop conceptual ethnographic frameworks for their collaborations.

Islands
O for God's sake
they are connected
underneath

They look at each other
across the glittering sea
some keep a low profile

Some are cliffs
the bathers think
islands are separate like them

Muriel Rukeyser[1]

Introduction

In this article, we present a "telling case" (Mitchell, 1984) of an interdisciplinary, team-teaching experience that explores how participants eschewed *ethnocentricism* of their fields of study in order to learn from each other, while providing instruction to students and analysing data collected from the class (a graduate course on literature and pedagogy). Through this process, the participants (a professor of English education and a professor of literature) initially ground the perspectives of literary interpretation in their field of study or discipline but eventually developed a conceptual framework that guided their interactions and analysis of the discursive actions of the class. An ethnographic perspective served as the conceptual frame and informed how the participants observed, described and developed claims about classroom interactions. Through this study, we answer calls for more examples of how faculty in higher education engage in interdisciplinary teaching and research (e.g. Friedow, Blankenship, Green, & Stroup, 2012; Paulus, Woodside, and Ziegler, 2010; McMurtry et al., 2012; Spelt, Biemans, Tobi, Luning, & Mulder, 2009) and the need for faculty to develop conceptual frameworks for their collaborations.

Although we are both professors in the departments of English language and literature, respectively, at a state university, we are associated with different programs that are named according to the academic discipline (literary studies) and the field of study (education). Our interest initially focused on how our different scholarly backgrounds mutually informed a common topic: how graduate students – most of them teachers – engage in literary interpretation and the consequences of their assumptions and literacy practices for their students. We grew interested in how interdisciplinary conversations led to epistemological explorations and literacy practices that helped us to create a shared framework, one that made visible connections between apparently separate islands of our fields of study, a metaphor captured in Rukeyser's poem, while recognizing the value of each.

We agreed that there was no single authoritative body of knowledge on literary interpretation and pedagogy, and our discussions heightened our recognition of the social construction of disciplinary knowledge, as Kelly, Green, and Luke (2008) describe: through participating "in the discourse and actions of a collected social field ... knowledge is not held in archives and texts, but is constructed through ways of speaking, writing and acting. Thus, knowledge is continually tested, contested, and reconstructed through the emerging genres of academic knowledge in education" (p. ix). Based on these premises, how would we negotiate differences that might emerge from our academic fields or disciplines and institutional expectations in order to examine our interests and practices in how we train teachers in literary interpretation?

Disciplines or fields of study as *languacultures*

Discipline-based scholarship is a core value of colleges and universities, evidenced by funding, rewards, and publications, although some institutions have reshaped their systems to include a wider range of what constitutes scholarship, including teaching (O'Meara, 2005). A comprehensive discussion of the contested terms of *disciplines* or *disciplinarity* is beyond the scope of this paper; however, we turn to Krishnan (2009) for general criteria for academic disciplines: they have a "particular object of study," "a body of accumulated specialist knowledge referring to their object of research," theories and concepts that help to organize the knowledge, specific terminology or discourse, and particular research methods, and "some institutional manifestation in the form of subjects taught at universities or colleges, respective academic departments and professional associations connected to it" (p. 9). Disciplines are "defined not only by certain forms or bodies of *knowledge* but also certain *practices*" (Kreber, 2009, p. 24).

However, disciplinary perspectives at times fail to account for selected phenomena that appear outside of the boundaries of the discipline (Nissani, 1997), and borrowing between or among disciplines can be interpreted as "boundary work" (Klein, 1996). Yet disciplines purporting to examine similar phenomena appear to conflict, use different discourse, methods of inquiry, and forms of evidence, particularly for the purposes of accountability within disciplinary-based communities. From this perspective, disciplines can be viewed as silos within college or university, a recent metaphor, "probably most often associated with grain storage," suggesting an ignorance of developments in other fields and "the distance between university life and 'the real world'" (Jacobs, 2013, p. 18). Of course, as Jacobs points out, the challenges faced by disciplines (e.g. communicating to others outside of the discipline, including research partners) are pertinent to discussions of interdisciplinarity.[2] Most importantly for our purposes, work between disciplines or fields of study implies interactions between or among people, and disciplines can be viewed in ways parallel to cultures, or to what Michael Agar (1994, 2006) calls *languacultures*, a combination of discourse and culture, specifically the language used and constructed by a group within particular contexts over time.

Agar (1994) states, "The *langua* in languaculture is about discourse, not just about words and sentences. And the *culture* in languaculture is about meanings that include, but go well beyond, what the dictionary and the grammar offer" (p. 96). Implicitly, this suggests that people of two cultures (or in our case, disciplines or fields of study) might appear to share a construct or topic of interest (e.g. literary interpretation); however, the history, theories, and assumptions of that construct or topic might differ greatly, although that might not be immediately apparent. According to Agar, *rich points* are likely to appear; that is, moments when something happens and participants suddenly "don't know what's going on" between them (p. 106). At these moments, there is potential to explore the rich point, to examine the possibilities of meaning, especially by trying to understand each other's perspective. Through these potential actions, according to Agar, participants are "building culture"; that is, "building new knowledge born of personal experience, a new awareness, [and] a new connection" (p. 107). His position raised questions for us as teachers and as researchers.

- How can participants from different languacultures or disciplines and fields of study recognize opportunities of rich points?
- How might participants reshape an interaction from one of confusion to one that explores differences and examines what differences those differences make (Green et al., 1996)?
- In particular, how can teachers or researchers observe rich points of interdisciplinary conversations and develop a logic of inquiry to see the differences and the potential consequences for addressing them?

Perspectives on challenges of interdisciplinary collaborations in higher education

Although interdisciplinarity is not necessarily preferable to disciplinarity – rigorous study in disciplines is critical for effective interdisciplinary collaborations (Jacobs, 2013), complex problems often demand knowledge from more than one field or discipline and students are implicitly expected to make connections between or among disciplines and learn how to apply such knowledge. Yet, instructors' different epistemologies, discourses, and approaches to teaching might differ and constrain the apparent opportunities for learning (Spelt et al., 2009), particularly if there is little or no room to discuss the apparent conflicts. McMurtry et al. (2012) state, "one cannot, and should not, attempt to avoid or eliminate these conflicts: 'difference, tension, and conflict are not barriers that must be eliminated. They are part of the character of interdisciplinary knowledge negotiation'" (p. 464). In other words, exploring and negotiating "difference, tension, and conflict," or rich points, are key practices that can effectively lead to new understanding and can demonstrate the value of interdisciplinary work and teaching.

Institutions of higher education increasingly include interdisciplinary collaboration as part of their strategic plans, although how to define the construct or describe the related processes and practices, or how faculty will most productively engage across intellectual traditions, is obscured (Friedow et al., 2012; Nowacek, 2007, p. 370). There is no template for initiating, negotiating and forming interdisciplinary teams that might provide benefits to all partners, including students. Three representative studies demonstrate a range of perspectives on interdisciplinary collaborations in higher education and point to dilemmas of recognizing apparent tensions, conflicts, or rich points as opportunities for negotiating new understandings.

McMurtry et al. (2012) examined the failed initiative of an interdisciplinary research collaboration. The six authors, who had participated in the original study, recognized the assumption that interdisciplinary approaches potentially lead to something different than using only one discipline or field of study, "that 'the sum is greater than the parts'" (p. 464). However, epistemological differences might circumvent the process, and they point to three criteria to address these types of differences: (1) developing a "conceptual frame," (2) using models that "typically include steps like defining a question, determining relevant disciplines, negotiating roles, identifying conflicts, creating common ground, and so on," and (3) "having a specific, concrete focus" (p. 465).

In another study, Friedow et al. (2012) examined their interdisciplinary collaboration in designing a graduate course focused on statistical literacy and instruction with an emphasis on writing. Three of the group members were from statistics and one was from the English department. To accomplish the task of developing the course, they came to realize the importance of three criteria. First, they had a shared goal of designing the class and negotiated their "different institutional and disciplinary positions in this new group" (p. 408), including preconceptions that group members may have had about the other's discipline, which enhanced their "interdisciplinary relationships" (p. 409). Next, they learned how their "respective disciplinary, subdisciplinary, departmental, and personal commitments to teaching and learning influenced the process of designing the syllabus of developing, enacting, and sustaining interdisciplinary pedagogy" (p. 414). They recognized that their disciplines had different ways of approaching problem solving, and exploring differences led them to "discuss their [disciplinary ways of problem solving] benefits and limitations in order to make strategic decisions about how they may or may not inform the course" (p. 410).

They found that effective collaboration for them meant "a willingness to see moments of difficulty and discomfort that arise in this process not as 'failed' pedagogical interactions but as opportunities for productive dialogue and further pedagogical inquiry" (p. 406). This finding is similar to Agar's description of *rich points* and the opportunities they provide for exploration and examination, particularly for the purposes of intercultural or interdisciplinary understanding. Finally, they describe the importance of inhabiting "a learner's stance," including on-going conversations about teaching, about disciplinary assumptions, and methods of instruction.

In a third study, Paulus et al. (2010), who represent three disciplines, examined their interdisciplinary approach as qualitative researchers by analysing audio conversations of their research process. Their analysis led to the recognition of three categories of assumptions that underlay their collaboration: positioning, meaning making and producing (p. 855). They describe how they oriented themselves as "learners not experts," making observations of the literature of the field for their study, noting their shared history and pointing to "outside authority" that sits in judgment of [their] work; these examples of how and what they positioned through dialogue represent the iterative process of their collaborative research, particularly how they constructed meaning over time. They view the group as having ownership over the writing they produced, not individual ownership of parts, and this awareness demonstrates how their "interpretations take a step toward exploring what is typically hidden in research reports – the collaborative conversations underlying the research process" (p. 858). Similar to Friedow et al., these researchers adopted a "learning stance" and observed their collaborative approach to "position taking, meaning making and producing."

The "telling case" (Mitchell, 1984) we present provides another example of collaboration, especially in terms of learning to see and hear, raise questions, and negotiate understanding from different perspectives. As in the cited studies, we adopted an inquiry stance on a particular topic, literary interpretation and the preparation of teachers, viewed ourselves as learners, and strived to adapt an ethnographic perspective as a conceptual frame to help us observe, describe, and analyse interactions with each other and the participants of our team-taught class.

Layers of context: constructing reflexive dialogues

The context for this study is a team-taught, graduate course that we designed for purposes of exploring practices of literary interpretation with teachers (graduate students) from (inter)disciplinary perspectives. The College of Arts and Sciences awarded us a grant to teach the course, and we elected to construct a graduate course because we wanted to engage in discussions of interpreting literature with experienced readers and teachers. There were two main reasons for this choice. First, we planned to make visible to participants our instructional decisions in selecting texts, initiating classroom practices, and conducting research for multiple purposes. The course would also provide us with opportunities to examine how the assumptions, theories, and practices of the class might inform how our department prepares teachers for the classroom.

At our comprehensive, public university, teacher candidates seeking certification to teach English as a subject area must take seven courses in literature, including one that introduces them to literary theory. Faculty trained in literary studies teach these courses. Prior to their field experience, candidates take an instructional methods course taught by the English Education faculty, and the class includes exploring assumptions and practices of interpretative theories. Although literature and English Education faculty are housed in the same department, they do not typically consult with one another about how candidates are trained as interpreters of literary texts or how candidates should design curricular approaches for secondary school students. However, because of our institutional proximity, we recognized the potential for interdisciplinary conversations and the potential value of these for students.

Our interest in interdisciplinary conversations centred on two previous observations. First, students experience literature courses as readers of texts within the literary studies program; that is, the classroom experiences as readers are designed by literature faculty whose discipline-based perspectives inform decisions on sequencing courses, selecting authors, time periods and textual issues, and preparing students for graduate studies. Yet, the *teaching* of literature is the purview of the secondary methods course and its faculty. There are no structural, curricular opportunities for students to discuss how the two experiences might transform them as interpreters of literary texts or as teachers of these texts. In other words, teacher candidates must figure out how the different disciplinary experiences might inform their curricular choices for secondary school students and to recognize gaps in their making such connections. We wondered how students negotiated apparent gaps, or rich points, between the experiences in literature and methods courses and how we could develop a metadiscourse that would make the links transparent and encourage (inter)disciplinary dialogues beyond informal, hallway conversations.

For the course we designed, "Reading, Interpreting and Responding to Literature" (a title negotiated among faculty of both programs), we intended to create dialogical spaces and to encourage students to initiate topics for discussion (e.g. via blogs, classroom discussions, research essays, etc.); to create an environment in which we were all learners, students, and teachers; to model and challenge positions of authority within representative fields of study; and to initiate a dialogue between English Education and Literary Studies that would lead to a discourse that might be described as interdisciplinary. We became conscious of disciplinary differences and sought to make visible the often-invisible contextualization cues (Gumperz, 1992) that lead to (mis)understanding and rich points. Our growing awareness of how our interactions were shaping our perspectives in preparation for a proposed course also demonstrated a practice of reflexivity, an important aspect of ethnographic and qualitative research (Pillow, 2003).

Methods: ethnographic perspective as a frame for interaction and research

An interactional ethnographic perspective (Castenheira, Crawford, Dixon, & Green, 2001; Green, Skukauskaite, & Baker 2012) guided the collection and selection of records and analysis of data. Anderson-Levitt et al. (2006) describe ethnography as a philosophy of research, and Green et al. (2012) similarly define ethnography as epistemology and outline the principles of a system that can be described through four criteria. First, the methodological approach is non-linear, one that is iterative and recursive and uses abductive logic. Next, the researcher leaves aside *ethnocentricism*; that is, the researcher does not presume but seeks to gather and record the life of the selected group and ground assumptions in discursive actions of the group, checking with members to ensure accuracy and striving to gain an "insider's perspective." Finally, the researcher identifies the boundaries of the phenomenon observed and builds connections among the bits in order to construct claims. Since we have approached the instruction and analysis of it from different disciplinary perspectives, the second of the criteria proved most essential.

One of our steps in avoiding ethnocentricism in analysing classroom interactions and preparing for each class session was to transcribe each class meeting because the document provided a way for us to ground observations in the discourse, not in our assumptions based on previous or disciplinary experiences. Instead of making assumptions about what we thought transpired in the class, we were able to read and discuss the transcript. The discourse was transcribed into message units, bursts of talk among participants that contributed to an understanding of the context of the discourse, including aural contextualization cues, which provided a way to examine the sequences of interactions or interaction units (Green & Wallat, 1981).[3] We would then observe how the class meeting separated into events.

Bloome, Carter, Christian, Otto, and Shuart-Faris (2005) define an *event* as "a bounded series of actions and reactions that people make in response to each other at the level of face-to-face interaction," and keys to the interactions are the linguistic processes used (p. 6). After transcribing each class meeting, we created charts, or *event maps*, that included the event, the clock and audio recorder time, the sequence of actions that occurred, and observational notes. Discourse analysis, including microanalysis of selected transcripts, led us to examine interactions and what was in the process of being constructed over time, including intertextual links that become resources for learning (Bloome & Egan-

Robertson, 1993; Bloome et al., 2005). In describing how intertextual links become resources for learning, Bloome and Egan-Robertson (1993) state: "A juxtaposition must be proposed, be interactionally recognized, be acknowledged, and have social significance" (p. 308). These criteria proved useful to us as instructors and as researchers.

Therefore, through the transcription and analysis of a class meeting before the next one, we were in the process of accomplishing three goals: (1) to examine the events of the class and gain insights into how the classroom discourse reflected what was being accomplished, including social and literacy practices of the group; (2) to reflexively prepare curricular opportunities that built on previous class meetings; and (3) to build an archive of records that we could consult, particularly so we could see links among events across time. Although we recognized the ethnographic perspective and analysis of discourse as resources for our instructional choices (cf. Rex & Schiller, 2009), we also began to see the value of it as people working together from different disciplines, as researchers and as teachers: an ethnographic perspective not only provided a framework to collect, archive and select records, construct and analyse data, it also contributed to our increased reflexivity as a team by forming the basis for an unfolding, common theoretical frame.

Bloome et al. (2005) state, *increased reflexivity* refers to "conducting research with an awareness of translation issues and of how the discourse of research and related academic discourses may influence or perhaps impose an interpretation on the experiences captured through research" (p. 48). What is intriguing to us is how Bloome et al. link the issue of translation to "power relations between researchers" and describe the value of "a reflexive stance as important to excavating power relations in classroom language and literacy events because it is not just the power relations among teachers and students, administrators, school boards, politicians, and so on, that are at issue but also the relationships of social institutions such as schooling, business, government and educational research" (p. 166). In our case, increased reflexivity helped us observe the relationships, and potential power issues, among our students and us, among programs within our department, and the disciplinary assumptions that informed how we approached literary interpretation in the class.

Telling case of a rich point as an opportunity for learning

In this section, we describe and analyse selected discursive actions in a sequence of events as a telling case of a team-teaching experience to explore how the actions reflected a dialogic, reflexive stance and how we recognized and uncovered a rich point that became an opportunity for learning. According to Mitchell (1984), "Case studies are the detailed presentation of ethnographic data relating to some sequence of events from which the analyst seeks to make some theoretical inference" (p. 237). In order to describe and demonstrate selected practices of a group, a researcher might select a "typical" case from among the data collected over time; however, Mitchell argues that selecting a "telling" case might be more fruitful in making "previously obscure theoretical relationships suddenly apparent" (239).

Sequence of classroom events

One example rich point that emerged from our discussions focused on a metaphor, "literary lenses," for describing literary theories. In the secondary methods course students are often encouraged to view different literary theories as "lenses" (e.g. Appleman, 2009; Carroll with English Education Graduate Students at Florida State University, 2006; Troise, 2007); however, Elisabeth questioned the accuracy or usefulness of the metaphor.

INTERDISCIPLINARY AND INTERCULTURAL PROGRAMMES

What follows is a four-part sequence of events that can be described as socially constructed intertextual links, which occurred over two class meetings. We selected this sequence because it reflects the transparency of instructional methods that we sought to share with the students, the reflexive approach that led to curricular decisions, and the rich point. It also exemplifies the ethnographic perspective and microanalysis of a key interaction that made the example rich point visible.

First classroom event on 13 February

During the first event on 13 February, the fifth class meeting, a guest speaker (via Skype), Dr. K, an English educator and literary scholar, warned teachers against "artificial" means of preparing students to read a text (e.g. a novel); that is, teachers should reject methods that "predetermine the interpretation of the text" (Audio Record, 00:16:57), basically any approach that leads students to consider particular perspectives or interpretations without first reading and discussing the text. He suggested that students engage in activities that encourage them to "point" to interesting or challenging aspects of the text, raise their own questions about sentences or lines in the text, and seek plausible answers through class discussion and rereading for clarification, among other practices. According to Dr. K, one of the goals for teachers should be to guide students to recognize that "[students] can read stories and have something to think about/and what they think counts/and their questions count," and to develop habits of experienced readers (e.g. Blau, 2003). He urged teachers to create space for students to engage in debate around the lines of a text.

Dr. K suggested that we use Kate Chopin's "The Story of an Hour" as an example short story that raises questions about gender and marriage at the turn of the twentieth century and has the potential to ignite debate. Although teachers' past literary experiences might typically lead to traditional interpretations of Chopin's story, the readers' developing theoretical perspectives and personal experiences would generate debate and potentially challenge those interpretations.

Final classroom event on 13 February

During the final ten minutes of the 13th February class meeting, Doug read aloud a children's story, Babette Cole's *Prince Cinders*, a picture book that parodies the story of Cinderella. The text offers a potentially controversial reversal of gender roles that challenges the interpretation of the traditional story and encourages readers to (re)consider how their background experiences and knowledge lead to particular interpretations (cf. Mellor, Patterson, & O'Neill, 1991). One of the reasons for reading the text was to build on practices suggested by Dr. K earlier in the class and to raise the issue of "literary lenses" as a metaphor.

The reading of *Prince Cinders*, and Doug's suggestion before reading it aloud to consider a "feminist lens," led to Elisabeth's reflection on the potential usefulness of the metaphor and its constraints and to an intertextual link made by one of the students. Elisabeth described the use of lenses as a "heuristic device…/to help students/…/[although] 'knowing a lens' is a little artificial actually/…/it's really Just something to teach theory/it's not really/how individual theorists necessarily/interact with texts" (13 February, lines 107–128). Rather, she says, "most people use like a kaleidoscope/you know do different things at the same time" (lines 129–130). One of the students, Marie, pointed to a connection to Dr. K's discussion about leading students: "[Literary lenses] seems kind of like what um/Dr. K was saying/directing the meaning they take from a text" (lines 134–137). She announced that she had had a

INTERDISCIPLINARY AND INTERCULTURAL PROGRAMMES

Classroom Events for 20 February					
Event 1 Announcements 12 min (00:00:00–00:11:59)	Event 2 "Reading Event*" 26 min (00:12:00–00:38:11)	Event 3 "Reading Event*" 22 min (00:38:12–1:00:28)	Event 4 Discussion of Research Projects 28 min (1:00:28–1:30:14)	Event 5 Break 16 min (1:30:14–1:46:41)	Event 6 Literary Lenses and The Story of an Hour 56 min (1:46:41–2:41:27)

*Each student led a *Reading Event* during the semester, selecting a text and engaging the class.

Event 6: Sub-Events				
Sub-event Unit 1: Class reads an excerpt of a transcript constructed for a discussion on literary theories from the previous class meeting (13 Feb); the content of the transcript provided a rationale for using *The Story of an Hour* by Kate Chopin.	Sub-event Unit 2: Doug leads class discussion and class listens to an electronic reading (from the Internet) of *The Story of an Hour*.	Sub-event Unit 3: A student initiates class discussion of *The Story of an Hour*: observations and interpretations. Nearly all present contribute to the discussion (11 of 14).	Sub-event Unit 4: "Rich point": Doug positions self as secondary reader and raises questions for teachers; Elisabeth provides literary reader perspective: "have a stake" in the discussion.	Sub-event Unit 5: Elisabeth leads class discussion about teaching and reading *The Story of an Hour*.
6 min (1:48:47–1:53:36)	10 min (1:53:37–2:02:46)	12 min (2:02:47–2:14:14)	7 min (2:14:16–2:20:33)	22 min (2:20:34–2:41:27)

Sub-Event 4: Interaction Units		
Interaction Unit 1: Doug and Elisabeth: *Rich point* emerges from Doug's question; Elisabeth responds that readers should "assume a stake" (2:14:16–2:17:43)	Interaction Unit 2: Elisabeth and Veronica: Student offers example and Elisabeth responds (2:17:44–2:17:58)	Interaction Unit 3: Doug and Elisabeth: Point to examples to support or expand ideas from "rich point" discussion (2:17:59–2:20:33)

Figure 1. Context for classroom interaction on "rich point" (20 February).
Note: Time is presented in minutes and digitally.

difficult time enjoying the story – in fact, "it kind of ruins the story/.../[because] the whole time I'm thinking/like/I'm trying to figure out/from a feminist perspective/what I should be offended by" (lines 144; 151–155).

Classroom event 6, Sub-event 1 on 20 February

For the 20th February class meeting, Doug and Elisabeth recontextualized (van Leeuwen, 2008) the interaction with Marie for the purposes of introducing Chopin's "The Story of an Hour" and encouraging further discussion on the metaphor of literary "lenses" (see Figure 1). That is, the transcription from the final classroom event on 13 February was used in the class to discuss the discourse that led from Elisabeth's observations about the metaphor of "lenses" for literary theories to Marie's observation and implicit understanding of a feminist lens.

Event 6, Sub-events 2–5 on 20 February

We chose to have "The Story of an Hour" read aloud by a free, online service (Sub-event 2), and we agreed that Elisabeth would lead the discussion because whole class discussions on literary texts were normal practices for her as a scholar and teacher (see Figure 1). (During the analysis of the event Elisabeth noted that managing the discussion put her into familiar territory and led her to feel more comfortable in the interdisciplinary environment.) After initial classroom observations of the text by students and instructors (Sub-event 3), a rich point emerged as Doug sought to shape the discussion towards pedagogy, raising questions about the purposes of a literary discussion and how Elisabeth viewed the role of theory during these types of interactions (Sub-event 4). Most importantly, he assumed the role of a secondary school reader and said, "As a reader/I'm reading something/[and] we start talking about it/and all of the sudden I can feel/[the interpretation] can be so many things/and I don't know where to go next/and I just start checking out" (see Table 1, lines 551–

INTERDISCIPLINARY AND INTERCULTURAL PROGRAMMES

Table 1. ***Rich point* interaction (20 February)** (Audio Recording Time: 2:14:16–2:17:43).

Speaker	Line	Message unit	Notes
Doug (2:14:16)	541	here's my question	Addresses Elisabeth
	542	here's my question to you especially	As literary scholar
Elisabeth	543	Ok	Signalling for D to continue
Doug	544	right about now is when I check out	Positioning self as a reader
Elisabeth	545	ok	Signalling for D to continue
All	546	[laughs]	
Doug	547	no	
	548	I'm enjoying [the discussion]	
	549	it's not you	i.e. Elisabeth
	550	it's not personal	Not a criticism of Elisabeth
	551	as a reader	Positioning self as reader
Elisabeth	552	yes	Signalling for D to continue
Doug	553	I'm reading something	For example
	554	we start talking about it	The text
	555	and all of the sudden I can feel	
	556	it can be so many things	i.e. the interpretation
	557	and I don't know where to go next	In terms of interpreting
	558	and I just start checking out	i.e. stop listening
	[…]		
	561	so my question partly is	
	562	where do you head with these kinds of stories [that people are telling during the interpretative event]	In other words, what does a reader (or teacher) do with the information offered?
	563	because I hear personal readings	
	564	I hear readings ground in the text for some purpose	
	565	I hear you know	
	566	there are so many things going on	During discussion
	567	so as teachers then how do we	From teacher's perspective
	568	it's not just for the teaching	
	569	because part of it	
	570	as a reader	
Elisabeth	571	yeah	Showing listening
Doug	572	what keeps your interest in	During discussions
	573	wanting to know something	
	574	and	
	575	as a teacher then	
	576	what *kinds* of things	i.e. practices
	577	should we be trying to do to	
	578	help people either to retain interest	
	579	*or*	
	580	*see* that what they are thinking	
	581	is something *worth* pursuing	
	582	because when you said	
	583	one thing that struck me was	
	584	when you said	
	585	to give a historical reading	Earlier in the discussion
	586	like Kelli proposed	
	587	so right away I'm thinking	
	588	that there are ways of proposing interpretations	During discussion
	589	and there are not uh	
	590	like a demand to find something	

(*Continued*)

Table 1. (*Continued*).

Speaker	Line	Message unit	Notes
	591	and I think that sometimes in the classroom	
	592	we know that at five til class is over	i.e. five minutes remaining
	593	I've heard many teachers say	
	594	"I want to make sure they know this before they leave"	
Elisabeth (2:15:50)	595	well what I would answer to this	
	596	and this is a very interesting question actually	
	597	because I think what you're saying	Reshaping D's question
	598	when we open up all these different ways of reading	
	599	they all seem equally possible	
	600	what do we do with that	Raises question
	601	[pause]	
	602	do we say	
	603	'ok very good	Claps and rubs hands together symbolizing, "we're done"
	604	'we have different ways of reading	
	605	"let's go home"	
	606	and if it's real life	Shifts to example
	607	you're not *really* satisfied with that	
	608	huh?	Rhetorical question
	609	if you are in an argument with your spouse	For example
	610	and he [or she] says "I saw this going on"	
	611	and you say "no, that went on"	
	612	you don't say	
	613	'all right	
	614	[pause]	
	615	'good	
	616	'you have your view and I have mine	
	617	"let's just go and do something else"	
	618	no!	Emphatic
	619	you want to say *"I'm right and you're wrong"*	Voice rises; Doug and some students laugh
	620	don't you?	Rhetorical question
	621	'and this is what you don't see	Continuing with example
	622	"and if you saw it my way you would also see that differently"	
	623	so	
	624	you want students to assume a stake in a particular interpretation	Main point
	625	huh? [voice rises]	Rhetorical question

558). In other words, he suggests that readers can feel overwhelmed with interpretative possibilities and might stop participating in the group discussion.

Elisabeth answers by stating one of the key practices that she, as a literature professor, wants her students to demonstrate: "You want students to assume a stake in a particular interpretation" (Table 1, line 624); however, she concludes by acknowledging, "I think that's the point we don't often get at it/.../[because] as a teacher you also don't know quite what to do with that" (lines 642–644). That is, teachers do not always know how to negotiate the multiple possibilities presented and to urge students (often 30 or more) to have a stake in a particular interpretation. Following the interaction between the two instructors, more students began to comment on various aspects of the story and the potential for teaching it or incorporating literary theory (Sub-event 5).

Discussion

Figure 1 provides a graphic (re)presentation of the event structure of the class on 20 February (the sixth class meeting). As indicated in the top table of Figure 1, the class session was divided by content into six events – included are the minutes and digital numbers from the audio recorder devoted to each. During Event 6, the class focused on literary "lenses" as a metaphor for engaging with different literary theories on the reading and interpreting of "The Story of an Hour", and on questions about observed interactions or potential literacy practices in secondary school classrooms. Through the analysis of the classroom discourse, the event showed five sub-events (see Figure 1, middle table).

In the first sub-event, class participants discussed an excerpt of a transcript from a discussion on literary theories during the previous class meeting (13 February). Next, Doug clarified the purpose of using the story by making links to the previous class meeting, and then the class listened to an electronic reading (from the Internet) of the story. When the reading concluded, Elisabeth and Doug offered brief comments about the version of the reading. Then one of the students, Emily, refocused the conversation on the content of the story, beginning observations and interpretations to which nearly all members (11 of 14) of the class contributed.

As the discussion paused for a moment, Doug positioned himself as a secondary school reader participating in a class discussion of a literary text, "right about now is when I check out" (Table 1, line 544). This statement generated a "rich point" because he turned towards Elisabeth, a literary scholar used to leading similar discussions in her courses, and wondered about the purpose of such conversations. However, instead of literally "checking out" (i.e. stopping to participate), Doug states that the class discussion presents many observations and perspectives, yet the interpretation of the story "can be so many things" (line 556) that the next steps as a participant – and the purpose of the discussion – is often unclear. He then shifts to a teacher's perspective and raises a question that is relevant to the students, most of whom are teachers: "As a teacher then/what kinds of things [i.e. practices]/should we be trying to do [with students] to/help people either to retain interest/ or/see that what they are thinking/is something worth pursuing?" (lines 576–581). Doug then hands over the discussion leader role to Elisabeth.

Elisabeth provides a rationale for interpretative discussions of literary texts: "you want students to assume a stake in a particular interpretation" (line 624). It is important to note that the wait time between Doug and Elisabeth was about one second; therefore, students did not have time to answer the question that Doug posed without interrupting. After a brief interaction between Elisabeth and a student (Veronica), Doug and Elisabeth provide examples to further discuss the value and necessity of "having a stake" in a discussion of literary texts.

Through nearly all of Sub-event 4 of Event 6, only Doug and Elisabeth talked; although the students were present they did not verbally interact in this sequence. Given that the event was audio recorded, not video recorded, an obvious question emerges: what evidence is there that students were engaging in the discussion? Analysis of Sub-event 5 provides evidence of issues students were interested in; five interaction units were observed and Elisabeth participated in all of these, demonstrating further her leadership of the sequence of interactions. Through discourse analysis, three main types of responses became visible in the interactions: (1) observations and descriptions of experiences of literary discussions among secondary students and teachers (e.g. Maha described reactions of students to a teacher who controlled the interpretative event), (2) proposed literacy practices and class interactions among secondary students (e.g. Debra wondered about how to engage students in her class of alternative school students), and (3) interpretations of "The Story of an Hour" (e.g. Tim continued to propose thematic interpretations). The diversity of responses provides evidence that students were welcome to contribute to the topic of discussion or to link with an earlier event (e.g. Tim began raising interpretative questions in Event 3). In other words, the students' responses visible in Sub-event 5 demonstrate what had become available to students for either entering a discussion on a current topic or shifting to their own topics of interest.

Conclusion

The choice of these events demonstrates conscious decisions on our part as instructors and as researchers. Through audio recording and transcribing much of each class, and then observing and discussing the transcript or portions of it from an ethnographic perspective, we show part of the reflexive process of developing a conceptual frame that encouraged us to observe, describe, and point to key moments or sequences. Instead of evaluating class events, students' responses, or instructional choices from our disciplinary points of view or past experiences, we sought to observe and describe what was happening in the class from an ethnographic perspective, grounding observations and claims in the discourse of participants. By sharing an example transcript and our interactional process with the class, we were striving to make transparent the rationale for curricular choices (e.g. the selection of "The Story of an Hour") and to model an approach to conversations between our fields of study and us. Furthermore, we strived to reveal opportunities and challenges of a dialogic, reflexive interdisciplinary collaboration.

The ethnographic framing of our conversations around 13 February events led us to ground observations in the transcript, to describe what we noticed, and to avoid relying on ethnocentric assumptions about what was said and for what purposes. However, this process was not easily established during the interactions of Event 6 on 20 February, mainly because the interactions were in real time, and the transcript shows evidence of the diplomacy required. For example, at the critical moment when the rich point was emerging, Doug reassured Elisabeth publicly that his question was "not personal"; rather, he was positioning himself as a student. In turn, Elisabeth recognized the question as urging a disciplinary response as to the value or purpose of literary discussions around a text, "you want students to assume a stake" in the conversation, to take a stand, to debate, and to use evidence for claims. We clearly recognized the rich point and we resolved it as an intertextual link (i.e. one that was interactionally recognized, acknowledged, and socially significant) only through the analysis of the event. (In fact, through the analysis of this sequence, we observed another rich point, one we did not pursue. On 13 February, Elisabeth stated that literary scholars do not really use "lenses" of particular theories; rather, they use multiple theories, depending on the purpose; and her response surprised Doug because of her apparent dismissal of a term accepted in the discourse of English education.)

The exchange between us during Event 6 publicly demonstrated the dialogic and reflexive approach to the subject and our interdisciplinary inquiry: it began with our past experiences and disciplinary perspectives and moved towards discussion in an interdisciplinary space. Following the exploration of the rich point between Doug and Elisabeth, students began to respond, demonstrating their interest in the topic as teachers (e.g. Maha's and Debra's responses) and as readers of literary texts (e.g. Tim's response). However, this apparent agreement resolving the rich point does not necessarily signal a shift from disciplinary perspectives. As a secondary teacher or English educator, Doug focused more on how students react to instruction, how they understand the process of interpretation, what counts as interpretative practices; Elisabeth, on the other hand, focused more on interpretations offered, interpretative practices ("having a stake"), textual evidence presented, and the rationale for the stakes that underlie a reader's logic. The interdisciplinary space and interactions encouraged class participants to explore points of contention (e.g. rationale to use the metaphor of "lenses," or the purpose of literary discussions) from different perspectives, ones ground in different academic histories and theories.

Next steps

The key to analysing the discourse and classroom interactions discussed above rested on the fact that we had constructed transcripts from records collected and examined them from an interactional ethnographic perspective, which helped us to avoid ethnocentric assumptions of our disciplines and to form understanding through discussion and recognition of a rich point. We learned to appreciate the time-consuming work of interacting across disciplines and of making visible the emerging transdisciplinary practices that helped us to recognize connections. The process of our interdisciplinary collaboration and of working on this essay intensified our awareness of the crucial role of dialogue, in particular open-ended and reflexive dialogue, which allowed us to observe and discuss "what happened" in the dialogic spaces we created.

As part of our commitment to communicating across disciplines, we have come to realize the importance of learning about each other's discipline and field of scholarly specialization. There are limits to what we can be certain about, even in our own fields, especially when we seek knowledge and make claims about topics or issues in other disciplines (cf. Baker & Green, 2007). Moreover, because disciplines are constantly producing new knowledge and scholarly debates, it is challenging to stay abreast of one's own field. In order to participate in productive inter-, trans-, and disciplinary dialogues and collaboration, however, teaching each other – or learning about each other's – discipline becomes an important practice with benefits for mutual understanding and instruction. We leave this study with a couple of questions for instructors and for researchers.

- If disciplines are indeed "languacultures," as Agar proposed, and learning about each other's discipline is a form of intercultural exchange, how can we initiate, sustain, and observe spaces of active participation in these types of exchanges?
- And if an ethnographic perspective can provide a conceptual frame for participants of different languacultures working together, what other types of conceptual frames might participants, depending on their academic backgrounds, adapt or construct for the purposes of designing curricular opportunities for students or for conducting research?

Notes
1. Permission to use "Islands" by Muriel Rukeyser granted by William ("Bill") Rukeyser.
2. For distinctions among interdisciplinarity, multidisciplinarity, and transdisciplinarity, we turned to a literature review in a medical journal, a field where the terms are used often.

Multidisciplinary research elicits and builds on perspectives from different disciplines; interdisciplinary research seeks "a synthesis of two or more disciplines, establishing a new level of discourse and integration of knowledge"; and transdisciplinary research works "within and beyond disciplinary boundaries" for the purposes of leading to new perspectives (Choi & Pak, 2006, p. 355).
3. According to Green and Wallat (1981), the sequences of interactions between or among the members of the class, including the teachers, are composed of linguistic markers and content that the interactions cohere around. Similarly, interaction units are composed of message units, the bursts of speech of the interactants.

References

Agar, M. (1994). *Language shock: Understanding the culture of conversation.* New York, NY: William Morrow.

Agar, M. (2006). An ethnography by any other name. *Forum Qualitative Sozialforschung/Forum: Qualitative Social Research, 7,* 4.

Anderson-Levitt, K. (2006). Ethnography. In J. L. Green, et al. (Eds.), *Complementary Educational Research Methods.* Washington, DC: AERA.

Appleman, D. (2009). *Critical encounters in high school English: Teaching literary theory to adolescents.* Urbana, IL: NCTE.

Baker, W. D., & Green, J. L. (2007). Limits to certainty in interpreting video data: Interactional ethnography and disciplinary knowledge. *Pedagogies: An International Journal, 2*(3), 191–204. doi:10.1080/15544800701366613

Blau, S. (2003). *The literature workshop.* Portsmouth, NH: Heinemann.

Bloome, D., Carter, S. C., Christian, B. M., Otto, S., & Shuart-Faris, N. (2005). *Discourse analysis and the study of classroom language and literacy events.* New York, NY: Routledge.

Bloome, D., & Egan-Robertson, A. (1993). The social construction of intertextuality in classroom reading and writing lessons. *Reading Research Quarterly, 28*(4), 304–333.

Carroll, P. S., with English Education Graduate Students at Florida State University. (2006). Learning to view literature instruction with literary lenses: One group's story. *English Journal, 95*(3), 74–80. doi:10.2307/30047048

Castenheira, M. L., Crawford, T., Dixon, C., & Green, J. (2001). Interactional ethnography: An approach to studying the social construction of literate practices. *Special Issue of Linguistics and Education: Analyzing the Discourse Demands of the Curriculum, 11*(4), 353–400.

Choi, B. C. K., & Pak, A. W. P. (2006) Multidisciplinarity, interdisciplinarity, and transdisciplinarity in health research, services, education and policy: 1. Definitions, objectives and evidence of effectiveness. *Clinical and Investigative Medicine, 29*(6), 351–364. Retrieved September 30, 2014, from http://www.courseweb.uottawa.ca/pop8910/PDF%20Files/Choi_Multidisciplinary

Friedow, A. J., Blankenship, E. E., Green, J. L., & Stroup, W. W. (2012) Learning interdisciplinary pedagogies. *Pedagogy, 12*(3), 405–424. Retrieved May 26, 2014, Project Muse http://muse.jhu.edu.ezproxy.emich.edu/journals/pedagogy/v012/12.3.friedow.pdf

Green, J. L., Kelly, G. J., Castanheira, M. L. Esch, J., Frank, C., Hodel, M., ... Rodarte, M. (1996). Conceptualizing a basis for understanding: What differences do differences make? *Educational Psychologist, 31*(3/4), 227–234. doi:10.1080/00461520.1996.9653269

Green, J. L., Skukauskaite, A., & Baker, W. D. (2012). Ethnography as epistemology: An introduction to educational ethnography. In J. Arthur, M. Waring, R. Coe, & L. V. Hedges (Eds.), *Research methodologies and methods in education*. London: Sage.

Green, J. L., & Wallat, C. (1981). Mapping instructional conversations: A sociolinguistic ethnography. In J. L. Green & C. Wallat (Eds.), *Ethnography and language in educational settings*. (pp. 161–205). Norwood, NJ: Ablex.

Gumperz, J. J. (1992). Contextualization and understanding. In A. Duranti & C. Goodwin (Eds.), *Rethinking context* (pp. 229–252). Cambridge: Cambridge University Press.

Jacobs, J. A. (2013). *In defense of disciplines: Interdisciplinarity and specialization in the research university*. Chicago, IL: University of Chicago.

Kelly, G. J., Green, J. L., & Luke, A. (2008). What counts as knowledge in educational settings: Disciplinary knowledge, assessment, and curriculum. *Review of Research in Education, 32*, vii–x. doi:10.3102/0091732X07311063

Klein, J. T. (1996). *Crossing boundaries: Knowledge, disciplinarities, and interdisciplinarities*. Charlottesville: University of Virginia.

Kreber, C. (2009). The modern research university and its disciplines: The interplay between contextual and context-transcendent influences on teaching. In C. Kreber (Ed.), *The university of its disciplines: Teaching and learning within and beyond disciplinary boundaries*. New York, NY: Routledge.

Krishnan, A. (2009). *What are academic disciplines: Some observations on the disciplinarity vs. interdisciplinarity debate*. Economic and Social Research Council for Research Methods, NCRM Working Paper Series. Retrieved from http://eprints.ncrm.ac.uk/783/1/what_are_academic_disciplines.pdf

McMurtry, A., Clarkin, C., Bangou, F., Duplàa, E., MacDonald, C., Ng-A-Fook, N., & Trumpower, D. et al. (2012) Making interdisciplinary collaboration work: Key ideas, a case study and lessons learned. *Alberta Journal of Educational Research, 58*(3), 461–473 Retrieved from http://ajer.synergiesprairies.ca/ajer/index.php/ajer/article/view/1068

Mellor, B., Patterson, A. H., & O'Neill, M. H. (1991). *Reading fictions*. Urbana, IL: NCTE.

Mitchell, J. C. (1984). Case studies. In R. F. Ellen (Ed.), *Ethnographic research: A guide to general conduct* (pp. 237–241). Orlando, FL: Academic.

Nissani, M. (1997). Ten cheers for interdisciplinarity: The case for interdisciplinary knowledge and research. *The Social Science Journal, 34*(2), 201–216. doi:10.1016/S0362-3319(97)90051-3

Nowacek, R. S. (2007). Toward a theory of interdisciplinary connections: A classroom study of talk and text. *Research in the Teaching of English, 41*(4), May 368–401.

O'Meara, K. A. (2005). Encouraging multiple forms of scholarship in faculty reward systems: Does it make a difference? *Research in Higher Education, 46*(5), 479–510. doi:10.1007/s11162-005-3362-6

Paulus, T. M., Woodside, M., & Ziegler, M. F. (2010). "I tell you, it's a Journey, isn't it?" Understanding collaborative meaning making in qualitative research. *Qualitative Inquiry, 16* (10), 852–862. doi:10.1177/1077800410383124

Pillow, W. S. (2003). Confession, catharsis, or cure? Rethinking the uses of reflexivity as methodological power in qualitative research. *International Journal of Qualitative Studies in Education, 16*(2), 175–196. doi:10.1080/0951839032000060635

Rex, L. A., & Schiller, L. (2009). *Using discourse analysis to improve classroom interaction*. New York, NY: Routledge.

Spelt, E. H. J. Biemans, H. J. A., Tobi, H., Luning, P. A., & Mulder, M. (2009). Teaching and learning in interdisciplinary higher education: A systematic review. *Educational Psychology Review, 21*(4), 365–378.

Troise, M. (2007). Approaches to reading with multiple lenses of interpretation. *English Journal, 96*(5), 85–90.

Van Leeuwen, T. (2008). *Discourse and practice: New tools for critical analysis*. New York, NY: Oxford University Press.

Van Rijnsoever, F. J., & Hessels, L. K. (2011). Factors associated with disciplinary and interdisciplinary research collaboration. *Research Policy 40*(3), 463–472. Retrieved from May 25, 2011 from Elsevier, http://dx.doi.org.ezproxy.emich.edu/10.1016/j.respol.2010.11.001.

Challenging points of contact among supervisor, mentor teacher and teacher candidates: conflicting institutional expectations

Laurie Katz[a] and Zeynep Isik-Ercan[b]

[a]Department of Teaching & Learning, The Ohio State University, Columbus, OH, USA; [b]Department of Educational Studies, Indiana University-Purdue University Fort Wayne, Fort Wayne, USA

> Grounded in an ethnographic logic of inquiry utilizing the concept of languaculture, this study explores how cultural differences between a field-based team and the university supervisor led to unanticipated challenges and points of conflict in an early childhood teacher education program in Midwestern United States. By examining points of contact as points of cross-cultural interaction, researchers examine ways in which (a) cultural expectations proposed through the discourse-in-use of teacher candidates, mentor teacher, and university supervisory personnel made visible what counted as expected practices and (b) cultural differences in the inscriptions of the field-based actors and university program. Findings indicate that the field-based team (re)formulated and provided a rationale for what counted as appropriate ways of lesson planning and lead teaching. However, after providing extensive support for building the team, the university expectations returned to a static model, thus failing to accommodate to the needs of the team and mentor teacher. This study highlights how the roles and relationships among the triad need to become a focus particularly when new or innovation program designs are being undertaken. The results suggest that the dynamic roles and relationships among the triad need to become a focus particularly when new program designs are being undertaken. The study also calls for multiple angles of analysis of the demands and opportunities for different actors at points of contact across institutional boundaries.

Roots of and goal for the study

This study utilizes ethnography as a way of knowing, that is, as epistemology (Agar, 2012) and a philosophy or research (Anderson-Levitt, 2003) to better understand the points of contact among actors in a field-based team (i.e., two teacher candidates with one mentor teacher) and a university supervisor, all part of a graduate early childhood (pre-k–third grade) licensure program in the Midwestern United States. The initiative on teaming undertaken by this teacher preparation program is grounded in an inquiry orientation to inform the program design, content afforded to candidates, and school–university relationships. The inquiry orientation and findings of cultural clashes between the field-based team and university supervisor in an earlier study (Katz & Green, 2012) formed the basis for this second study, drawing on data from the ethnographic archive.

The first analysis (Katz & Green, 2012) traced a voluntary team of two teacher candidates as they engaged in their second student teaching placement working with one mentor teacher in an urban third-grade classroom. The study explored the roots of such cultural differences before the program decided to shift field experiences to a model of two teacher candidates with one mentor teacher from the traditional pairing of one teacher candidate and one mentor teacher, a shift design to address recent calls in the United States for models of collaboration versus supervisory among the members of the triad.

This second analysis was designed to provide further information about how the candidates worked with the mentor teacher and the unanticipated clashes that occurred during interviews about what counted as lesson planning and teaching to each group, that is, the university team (supervisor, teacher candidates, and program faculty) and to the field-based team (mentor teacher and teacher candidates). The analysis explored the clash in frames of reference (Tannen, 1979) of the field-based team with that of the university supervisor and how differences in roles and relationships led to a bidirectional challenge to both the field-based team and supervisor (and by extension, the program). The following reflection voiced by the university supervisor at the end of the program was an unanticipated finding identified in the original study (Katz & Green, 2012) and captures this clash: "The [field-based] team was functioning well to find their answers in planning and teaching. That is why what we [university-based team] require did not always fit what happened within [field-based] team dynamic" (p. 102). The tension emerged from the university supervisor viewing the candidates as successful in planning and teaching as a team, although university procedures and expectations were not followed.

Review of literature
Beginning in the 1980s a body of research explored cultural clashes within teacher education programs and field-based experiences in an effort to address school–university divides in the United States (Avalos, 2011). Challenges identified in attempts to bridge these two structures have been characterized as complex, due to differing epistemologies (Joram, 2007), that is, differing norms and values for what knowledge, practices, and understandings involved in becoming a teacher (Murray, Swennen, & Shagrir, 2009). At the centre of these attempts to reformulate school–university structures is a shift in the relationship among university educators, teacher candidates, and mentor teachers (LePage, Boudreau, Maier, Robinson, & Cox, 2001), although the specific names of these actors vary.

Underlying the need to rethink these relationships is the recognition that field experiences need to become sites for inquiry into the nature of such relationships (Cochran-Smith & Lytle, 2009; Schön, 1987), and improving teacher quality cannot be accomplished by maintaining isolated learning experiences occurring within only one of these institutional structures. Darling-Hammond (2010) argued such experiences require integrated opportunities for interacting and learning in which boundaries between school and university become fluid. She further argued participants may face unanticipated and ill-defined problems as they seek to blur boundaries between university work and field experiences, issues that are examined in the present study. The review of research presented in the next section examines literature that explored what occurs at points of contact between university and school and between the university's teacher preparation program and field-based teams, including teacher candidates and the mentor teacher.

Cultural clashes between field and the university

Recently, teacher education as a field began reexamining field experiences of clinical preparation in the United States and other countries, including Norway (Elstad, 2010), Australia (Rorrison, 2010), Kenya (Ochieng' Ong'ondo & Borg, 2011), and United Kingdom (Edwards, 2010). Events precipitating these endeavours included Grossman and McDonald's (2008) call for research in teacher education to return to sustained inquiry about the clinical aspects of practice and how best to develop skilled practice, and the development of the Blue Ribbon Panel from National Council for Accreditation of Teacher Education to restructure the preparation of teachers to improve teacher quality by reflecting teaching as a practice-based profession (NCATE, 2010).

In this context, the nature of the student-teaching triad, functions and roles of each actor, and the consistency and intensity of mentoring teacher candidates receive from teacher education programs become topics of international debate. Zeichner (2010) raised questions about how to conceptualize the paradigm underlying such relationships and argued: "The old paradigm of university-based teacher education where academic knowledge is viewed as the authoritative source of knowledge about teaching needs to change to one where there is a non-hierarchical interplay between academic practitioner and community expertise" (p. 89). This argument provides a partial explanation of one key source of the tension for the supervisor as well as the field-based team identified by Katz and Green (2012). The issues Zeichner (2010) raised, therefore, frames the need to explore how the roles and relationships among actors at points of intersecting institutional contexts make visible what counts as knowledge and who owns it.

Supervisory practices at the intersection

The perspectives and functions of one such actor, the university supervisor, within these intersecting cultures, is one area needing further exploration. Researchers emphasize the potential contributions of supervisors to the growth of new teacher skills, especially with regard to their ability to act as a mediator between the mentor teacher and teacher candidate (Koerner, Rust, & Baumgartner, 2002; Yusko, 2004). Supervisors typically represent and clarify the program's expectations and communicate the university's philosophy in the field (Koerner et al., 2002). They also provide pedagogical, emotional, and motivational support to teacher candidates (Koerner et al., 2002; Yusko, 2004). Scholarship is emerging regarding how supervisors negotiate field experiences and implement strategies for supporting individual teacher candidates, such as making explicit their tacit knowledge in contributing to teacher candidates' knowledge and skills (Slick, 1998; Yusko, 2004). For example, supervisors heavily draw from their own teaching experience while supervising teacher candidates (Cuenca, Schmeichel, Butler, Dinkelman, & Nichols, 2011) and negotiate these roles considering their past and current sociocultural experiences, which might include international supervision practices (Isik-Ercan & Kang, 2009).

Some researchers argue the concept of university supervision, particularly the supervisors' traditional role of evaluation, positions the university as an outsider, and therefore an artificial addition to the student teaching experience (Bullough & Draper, 2004; Slick, 1998). This pattern seems consistent throughout international studies as well (Ochieng' Ong'ondo & Borg, 2011). Furthermore, Zeichner (2010) argues that supervisors are often employed short-term and may lack specialized training in mentoring novice teachers. Similarly, in a study in an Emirates context, Ibrahim (2013) found that directive approaches to supervision are common, which might limit collaborative nature of teacher growth and make the division of field and university program stand out even more to teacher candidates. He concludes that when teacher candidates take on submissive roles, the supervisor's relationship to the teacher candidate constitutes one-way directions and expectations, which might negatively influence the latter's beliefs towards teaching as a profession. A similar pattern persists in a Kenyan study, which found supervision practices to be evaluative and authoritative (Ochieng' Ong'ondo & Borg, 2011), instead of empowering teacher candidates' autonomy or fostering collaborative analysis and decision-making. Fantozzi (2013) argues that while these strategies are still valuable for many teacher candidates as novice teachers who are anxious to be confirmed by a more experienced mentor, it might hinder their growth of "self-consciousness and self-reflection"-pertinent characteristics for assessing their own performance.

Recent studies offer alternative ways to think about supervision in a context where teacher candidates and mentor teachers form fluid and dynamic partnerships. Some ways to enhance supervisory experience include utilizing university faculty's experience for supervision (Beck & Kosnik, 2002), delegating both supervisor and mentor teacher roles to the classroom teacher in the name of "clinical-master-teacher", implying a shift towards practical knowledge (Wilson, 2006), having supervisors engage in dialogue with each other in learning how to use various supervisory techniques that are geared towards each teacher candidate's strengths and needs (Ibrahim, 2013), and creating third spaces of dialogue during reflective seminars on campus where a group of teacher candidates and supervisors together discuss pressing dilemmas in the field and sustain conversations, which might not have happened during official visits (Cuenca et al., 2011).

Researchers in an exploratory study in Canada (Hamel, 2011) implemented video-conferencing as a tool for supervisor/teacher candidate dialogue when teacher candidates were in remote locations. Also introduced was an electronic forum where groups of three teacher candidates lead and exchange ideas about different pedagogical beliefs, with the supervisor helping them to reflect on these ideas later and building on each teacher candidate's strengths. Both parties reported that this practice helped teacher candidates build their own professional identity. A French study using activity theory (Cartaut & Bertone, 2009) also explored joint reflective dialogues among the triad. In another French study, Chaliès, Bruno-Méard, Méard, and Bertone (2010) observed that the supervisor and mentor teacher were successful in providing teacher candidates with general rules of teaching but did not necessarily help them to make sense of these rules and make decisions about how to follow or adopt the rules in particular teaching situations. While the teacher candidates made personal judgments and decisions about the learned rule and ultimately misinterpreted or rejected some, the authors argue that in order to realize a community of learners model, the rules should be scrutinized through collaborative critique and reflection with the supervisor and mentor teacher. Similarly, Bates and Dritz (2009) found that teacher candidates thought of "mutual, reciprocal" conversations with their supervisor as helping them to critically reflect on their teaching, their identity, and justify their decisions as new teachers.

These types of alternative and collaborative models encourage supervisors and teacher candidates to understand each other's perspectives, create a sense of community that is sustained by deeper conversations, enable supervisors to refine their focus and feedback for visits, and emphasize a new goal: emerging professional identity of the new teachers, instead of institutional standards or uniform expectations. These collaborative models demonstrate that the roles of the supervisor, teacher candidates, and mentor teachers should be fluid and based according to ongoing needs of the field experiences, the university program and growth of the teacher candidates. Accordingly, this present study adds to the current research of student-teaching triads by examining points of contact among supervisors, teacher candidates and mentor teachers as points of cross-cultural interaction in order to reconceptualize these interactions in a way that is responsive to the field dynamics and supportive for teacher candidates.

Methodology

Research questions

The research questions focus on two recurring themes that were identified in the earlier study (Katz & Green, 2012): lesson planning and lead teaching. The recurring nature of these topics identified the need to explore how differences in frames of reference at points of contact (conferences, interviews, and email correspondence) supported or constrained perspectives on what counted as expected ways of planning and lead-teaching to the different actors.

(1) How, and in what ways, did actors (mentor teacher, candidates, and supervisor) inscribe their values, goals, and expectations in their frames of reference for observing and talking about lesson planning and teaching? We define *inscribing* an actor's perspective by making visible the discourse (e.g., spoken or written language) used and how the actor engages with the discourse or the discursive actions. Green et al. (1996) examine Strike's (1974) use of how "the expressive potential of a perspective is shaped by and shapes the goals, values, and purposes of the community that constructed, maintains, and in some instances, extends it" (p. 227). In other words, the choice of language by members of a particular community places limits on what can be discussed and what aspects can be described in and through that language. Thus, the choice of language inscribes a particular view and set of understandings about the phenomena under study. This brings a common language such as what counts as *learning how to plan* and *teach classroom curriculum* under scrutiny when the choice and use of language is from different communities.

(2) What unanticipated challenges associated with roles and relationships were identified in the interactions among actors? This study constitutes a *telling case* (Mitchell, 1984), making visible what has been previously unknown. In telling cases, individuals or groups can be selected as tracer units making visible what members need to know, experience (or not), and thus, understand, produce, or predict (Heath, 1982). In this telling case, information is made visible through analysis of intertextual links in the data; for example, written, electronic, and conversational texts juxtaposed to identify each of the actors' perspectives (Bloome, Carter, Christian, Otto, & Shuart-Faris, 2005)

Principles of operation

An interactive, recursive and abductive, and often non-linear approach through these texts led to unanticipated findings given the following principles of languaculture, roles of the researcher, and identification of rich points. The first principle, languaculture conceptualized points of contact between the school and university for this ethnographic analysis (Katz & Green, 2012). Agar (2006) defined languaculture as follows:

> ...a concept ... to remind readers ... using a language involves all manner of background knowledge and local information in addition to grammar and vocabulary.... Culture becomes visible only when differences appear with reference to a newcomer, an outsider who comes into contact with it.... What it is that becomes visible in any particular case depends on the *Languaculture 1* (LC1) that the newcomer brought with them, a newcomer who might be an ethnographer.... *Languaculture 2* (LC2) learning, like ethnography, is driven by *rich points*.... Rich points are those surprises, those departures from an outsider's expectations that signal differences between LC1 and LC2 and give direction to subsequent meaning. (p. 5)

Drawing on Agar's distinction between LC1 and LC2, we argue that the university supervisor, other university personnel, and the teacher candidates are part of one languaculture (LC1) and that the mentor teacher and teacher candidates constitute another languaculture (LC2), given their sustaining local relationships. As LC1, the supervisor can be viewed as a "newcomer" to LC2 bringing her own LC1 to the field-based team's languaculture. Thus, we adopted the concept of languaculture to conceptualize relationships between school and university actors at points of contact and analysed the rich points as the unanticipated challenges between these points of contact.

This conceptualization enabled university-based researchers to adopt a second principle of operation that Heath (1982) and Katz and Green (2012) calls "stepping back from ethnocentrism" – that is, stepping back from what they knew or assumed about the university program to explore the cultural, social, as well as historical (program specific) presuppositions of different actors at points of contact.

A third principle of operation involved identifying boundaries of units of analysis, which in turn required shifting the focal LC1/LC2 in the intersecting communities in conferences between the university representative(s) and field-based team. This principle of operation led to the identification of rich points (Agar, 2006) and then enabled us to trace backward and forward in time through the records to identify inter-related records in which points of differences or what we refer to as *clashes in frames of reference* could be explored. Each of these points of frame clash, therefore, served as an anchor for exploring different angles of analysis of the roles and relationships among actors, the referential meanings needed to understand local meanings of actions and practices, and consequences of differences for particular actors.

This logic-in-use process also framed the basis for meeting a fourth principle of operation; that is, the making of grounded connections across actors, times, and meanings of practices and processes. Through contrastive analysis and the explorations of historical or parallel documents, actions, or processes that supported each actor but that also clashed with and/or supported the perspectives of others, we identified referential ties that laid a foundation for building warranted accounts of sources of inter-institutional frame clashes.

Program contexts and actors

The actors participating in this telling case included two candidates. Amy and Brad (all names are pseudonyms) volunteered and were recruited from a cohort of 58 in the Early Childhood Teacher Licensing Program. They are European-Americans in their early 20s and have known each other since high school. Other actors were a European-American mentor teacher (Megan) in a third-grade classroom with 17 years of teaching in urban primary schools; a supervisor (Denise) with 3 years of teaching and 3 years of supervision in the program, who was also an international doctoral student focusing on early childhood and primary education; and a European-American Program Manager, Sarah, with 33 years of teaching in urban public primary schools and 7 years of managing this teacher education program. Oversight of the teacher candidates occurred by the supervisor, who, in turn, was supported by, and responsible to, the Program Manager.

Situating the actors within the teacher education program

The teacher education program had a developmental orientation, in which each of the four phases of the 14-month program introduced experiences contributing to the next program phase. Thus, by the time Amy and Brad entered the third-grade classroom for their second student teaching placement, they had extensive experience in planning lessons at the preschool level.

The process of learning to teach in both field placements involved an "immersion period". At these first points of contact candidates were introduced to (a) each placement within its school and community contexts; (b) mentor teachers' classroom organization and curricular approaches; and (c) classroom students' interests, strengths, and needs. Thus, the immersion period foreshadowed what they would experience in student teaching, preschool through primary. Candidates took university classes 3 days/week (Monday, Tuesday, and Friday) and taught in their field placement 2 days/week (Wednesday and Thursday). Full-time student teaching followed this configuration in both placements – 5 days for 1 week in preschool and 8 weeks in their elementary classroom. During the primary placement, given their participation in the teaming research, the two candidates were expected to take turns as lead teacher, in contrast to solo teaching models that were the program norm. Before entering the final field placement, these candidates had 9 months of opportunities to learn what the university program required in terms of lesson planning, taking responsibility for lead teaching, and being assessed using the Praxis III: Classroom Performance Assessments (Dwyer, 1994), which was used by the university supervisor in compliance with state and national licensing and certification processes.

Elementary field placement

Amy and Brad were assigned to a third-grade classroom as their elementary field placement. The classroom, composed of 12 girls and 13 boys, was in a kindergarten – sixth-grade elementary school, where the ethnic and socioeconomic composition reflected that of the surrounding community: 92% African-American and 8% European-American, with 88% receiving free or reduced lunch. Megan described this class as one of the most challenging in her 17-year career, a view she made visible to the teacher candidates. Her perspective of the class was also shared by the university supervisor and other program personnel. Given the challenges of this placement, the field-based team organized and implemented their classroom practices in a manner that would, later, create a rich point; that is, differences in perspectives of different actors about what counted as being the lead teacher and lesson planning in the student teaching experience.

Data collection

The data set drew on records of the ethnographic archive, collected during the third-grade student teaching placement between January and June (Katz & Green, 2012). Records included 24 classroom observations (conducted 1–2 times a week) with field notes focusing on lessons conducted by candidates as well as on interactions among team members; two sets of formal interviews conducted individually with the mentor teacher, each candidate, and supervisor at the beginning and end of the program; and additional informal interviews conducted across phases of the program. Interviews addressed (a) field-based activities; (b) participants' perceptions of the field experience teaming model; (c) how, and in what ways, the teaming model contributed to, or inhibited, growth and learning to become a teacher; and (d) what roles and responsibilities were shared by the mentor teacher and candidates during daily classroom activities. Formal interviews and audio-recorded records that had been transcribed were also identified, as were other artefacts, for example, field notes of classroom observations, lesson plans, email communications, the supervisor's written observations, researchers' reflective logs, assessment forms, and conference reports. The researchers (authors) were directly involved in the data collection; Denise, the university supervisor, acted as the guide to the languaculture of program supervision.

Findings

Contrasting frames of reference on lesson planning and teaching

To explore further the roots of differences in expectations about lesson planning and teaching, we analysed how members of the two languacultures, the university and field-based team, inscribed *teaming* and its relationship to lesson planning and teaching. By identifying how different actors inscribed relationships between self and teaching processes and practices, as well as expected program requirements, we explored what counted as lesson planning and teaching to each actor and used rich points to trace forward and backward across time, events, and resources. Following is an analysis of each actor's perspectives, as supported by Table 1, which chronologically lists some of the events analysed.

Field-based actors' perspectives

The earliest inscription about planning identified was in a meeting on 14 February between one of the researchers and Brad, a teacher candidate. In his response to her question about how the team engaged with planning, Brad made visible a systematic approach that he and Amy used in their planning process. Each week they met on Tuesday to generate ideas to discuss with their mentor teacher and on Thursday to discuss what had occurred and to begin planning from that reflection. He also delineated a separation of responsibility in planning – he planned Math and Amy planned Social Studies activities.

Brad's response explains the roles and relationships within the team, sources of those roles, as well as responsibilities for planning and teaching. The process described becomes a frame clash between the two languacultures: as part of LC2, the two are sharing responsibility for planning and teaching a part of the curriculum and particular students through the implementation of centre activities; however, these actions are not the norm of LC1, where each teacher candidate conducts his or her own planning and teaching for the class. Subsequent analysis led to further clarification by both candidates of their planning and teaching, located in log entries and a transcript of an interview on 29 May among the candidates, mentor teacher, and site-based researcher. In this interview, Brad and Amy jointly construct a description of their planning and teaching (i.e., co-teaching) in situ modifications of the process, and roles and relationships created to respond to student needs and third grade standards:

Table 1. Points of contact in relation to lesson planning and teaching.

Dates: points of contact	Points of contacts in relation to lesson planning and teaching	Context and meaning
14 February	Supervisor visits Amy and Brad. Three teachers bonding and making decisions together	Mentor teacher shares frustration because the curriculum slowed down as a result on community building. Amy and Brad still struggling with classroom management but practicing more and gradually adjusting
14 February	Program manager visits classroom	The team creating three learning centres in classroom
28 February	Supervisor observation	Supervisor beginning to see missing lesson plans for teaching from both candidates and scarce written reflections from Brad and emails him (4 March), asking more
7 March	Brad answers and sends his requested reflection	Brad makes great progress. Supervisor makes suggestions and adds ideas
28 April	Supervisor emails Brad	Responds to his latest reflection (27 April); sends him good sample lesson plans. Supervisor notices his lesson plans lack format and details
29 April	Supervisor emails Brad	Asks for current week's lesson plans. Brad emails supervisor last week's lesson plans
30 April	Brad sends current week's plans. Amy also sends her plans	Supervisor sees many missing pieces in thinking and thorough planning for lessons. Contacts program manager for feedback
1 May	Program manager emails supervisor with feedback	Agrees with supervisor's concerns that lesson plans need attention and it is difficult to assess who teaches what. Requests additional information
1 May	Supervisor visits Amy and Brad for observation	Talks with three individually on the scarcity of communication, absences from placement, changing student-teaching dates, leadership in planning
1 May	Supervisor begins an email conversation with program manager and faculty leader (1 May), then with mentor teacher and candidates (2 May)	Clarifies program requirements. Asks candidates to clarify what days each will lead plan/teach and each candidate's roles in the process. Program manager and faculty leader email back and add ideas and affirm the plan of action Mentor teacher emails and resists to clearly defining the "lead teacher" role during the instruction and suggests "co-teachers" (3 May) Denise confirms mentor teacher's ideas but insists on clarification of roles for assessment purposes (3 May)
4 May	Amy emails the interview dates and her absences	There is growing concern for Amy's absences impacting her work/teaching by supervisor and program manager

(Continued)

INTERDISCIPLINARY AND INTERCULTURAL PROGRAMMES

Table 1. (*Continued*).

Dates: points of contact	Points of contacts in relation to lesson planning and teaching	Context and meaning
6 May	Program manager emails Amy about her absences and policy for make-up	Amy experiencing frustration for why some of the days do not count for her "lead" teaching. Later contact showed that Amy had been going on job interviews, and action made visible to the researcher when Brad became lead teacher
11 May		Supervisor still has concerns about missing lesson plans and absences. Some lesson plans sent, but often late

Brad: We're co-student teaching from the centre that I was teaching yesterday. I took it to Amy. I said, "Amy, this is what they're not understanding. I would like to do this with tomorrow's centre". Created the worksheet and then we went about centres – scrap what she did. So that's where the co-student teaching comes in.... Yes, she planned the overall (curriculum) throughout the week and the lesson plans but it's "co" because I went to her and said this isn't working...let me take over this part for tomorrow and do this...

This process was further confirmed in Amy's, June 3, reflective log entry:

I think we were confused the whole time, just trying to figure out...because what works for us, what works for the kids, what works for the university, what needs to be get done. I think originally we thought we all three be working together. But then we found out that ... which makes sense, we all needed to have lead days, so that everyone has these lesson plans accounted for, then it got away from us all three working together, and it became more of what is this person's role, we know that you are planning the lesson then you should be the teacher.

What the texts of the three field-based actors reveal is that they developed an ongoing process of negotiating who would do what, when, and where, with whom, in response to what was observed in relationship to students in the developing activity. They also frame a systematic process for planning initial instruction that involved multiple levels of interaction among different configuration of actions. In these different texts, they demonstrated a particular approach to planning and teaching that made "sense" to them and where they were meeting the expectations of LC2. These findings were unanticipated by LC1 because the approach clashed with LC1's norms for adhering to procedures for learning how to plan and teach.

The supervisor's perspective

The challenge of not following LC1 procedures was raised for the supervisor in a 2nd May correspondence between the supervisor and mentor teacher. Denise details in this email message to Megan her discussion with Amy about lesson planning, pointing to areas not included and restating required elements for the university program not evident in planning documents.

INTERDISCIPLINARY AND INTERCULTURAL PROGRAMMES

> We understand the planning process is very dynamic and interactive among the team. There are meetings where the team plans together, our expectations will be that the lead person for the week would finalize the planning with details and make decisions as necessary, as well as carrying the main responsibilities and role delegation among the team about preparation.

This email made visible a frame clash between the actions by Brad and expectations of the supervisor based on the university template and guidelines. In this email, Denise stated Amy understood what was expected but Amy claimed the format the field-based team was using made "more sense" to her. Denise's failure to explore what Amy meant by "makes more sense" provided evidence of which languaculture counted as a basis for assessment, LC2's. It is important to note Denise begins this email by using the collective pronoun "we". Denise's use of "we" implicates another actor, the Program Manager, involved in decision-making. The supervisor worked with the Program Manager when a resolution was needed if the teacher candidates were not following through on required university procedures. Therefore, the use of "we" at the onset of this email indicates the content was a collective decision and that Denise was guided by the norms of the university languaculture, LC1.

The analysis of the frame clash for Denise provided a rich point for examining what was inscribed, who contributed to the communication being sent to the mentor teacher, and what norms different actors did not take up. However, the clash appeared to be invisible, except as a deficit assessment of performance (i.e., Amy did not know how to engage in lesson planning) since the roots of Amy's planning was not explored; however, a search of the archive identified a response on 3 May by the mentor teacher, Megan:

> Both Amy and Brad have made huge strides in earning the students' respect and in creating the balance needed to establish rapport and appropriate consequences. It should be noted in your plan that they function as co-teachers who support the instruction. I don't think that the term "helper teacher" is appropriate.

In this email, Megan emphasizes Brad and Amy's roles as co-teachers and not as helper teachers, and she delineates steps involved in responsive planning and how teaching depended on a negotiated process. This email also made visible how the roots of this process were grounded in her need to meet state standards for third grade as well as her selected approach to working with her diverse and challenging group of students.

Denise's 10 June log entry documented her understanding of the field-based team's competence in making pedagogical decisions and taking pedagogical actions.

> ...What we ask from our regular interns did not work in this situation. The interns were in a very dynamic team and changing roles, and responsibilities. Their roles and responsibilities they decided to take on in the beginning did not fit what actually happened.... We as university folks wanted to know the role divisions to ensure two of them gain multidimensional experiences, such as planning alone, teaching whole group, leading the classroom alone, as well as team teaching, co-teaching, and teaching in the groups. Yet, the team focused on changing student dynamics, classroom context, and meeting the needs of individual students.

What her entry inscribed was a tension between her observations of the teacher candidates in the field-based classroom and how to document that they met program goals. In acknowledging that the candidates met the intent of the program in the area of pedagogy and planning, even though they did not follow the format that was expected, Denise faced an unanticipated challenge that led to a (re)formulation of her relationship with the field-based team. In other words her role shifted from one of providing primary support and feedback on teaching and planning to one similar to that of an "administrator" (her term) of the university's guidelines and the competencies defined in the Praxis III Assessments.

Unanticipated findings related to different languacultures: on roles and relationships

A recurrent theme emerging from unanticipated findings related to Amy and Brad's membership in both LC1 and LC2. Analysis of findings demonstrated how the teacher candidates were trying to adhere to the LC1 norms for learning how to plan and teach in a classroom, but these norms clashed with Amy and Brad's LC2 membership in this third-grade classroom. Unanticipated findings involved changes within the relationships and responsibilities between the teacher candidates, their mentor teacher (field-based team) and their university supervisor. One of those unanticipated findings related to Denise's role in supervision of the teacher candidates. For example, Denise was expecting Brad and Amy would have similar supervisory teacher candidate relationships according to LC1 norms regarding lesson planning. However, the analysis showed that although the candidates thought it was important to learn how to develop a lesson plan, they found the sequence of writing lesson plans and giving them to the supervisor in advance unhelpful to their learning process for becoming a teacher. In her interview on 3 June, Amy states:

> ...and we talk about everyday ... what happened today ... what should we do tomorrow? ... It [parts for planning] never looks like this the next day. I never actually end up doing what I had planned because they didn't get it, (or)they really got it ... We're always talking about what can we do ... What should I do, and I'm going to them (the field-based team) what should I plan for tomorrow?

Similar to their mentor teacher, they perceived the function of the lesson planning as an ongoing process among the field-based team to meet the curricular needs of the students across time and events.

Frame clashes between the two languacultures further occurred as Amy and Brad engaged in the teaming process within the field-based classroom. Tracing back and forth through the data, it appeared that LC2's decisions to create learning centres in the classroom and roles for each of the members of the field-based team to address the curricular and management demands of the classroom raised further clashed with LC1's supervisory roles. Denise found the LC2 classroom format of the learning centres and co-teaching roles of this field-based team made it difficult to determine how each teacher candidate could competently design and lead lessons for the entire class. For example, Denise found she was unable to directly observe LC1 competencies in each of their lesson planning documents, her weekly observations and reflections between herself (as supervisor) and each candidate.

Recognition of LC2 teaming by Denise can be found in the email on 14 February (Table 1), in which she observed the teacher candidates and mentor teacher had "bonded and making decisions together". Additionally, during the period following March 4 through the end of the program, analysis of data suggested the LC2 team was working well and no longer needed direct intervention from the supervisor or program manager. The data trail from 4 March focus on "meeting the requirements" of LC1 in terms of lesson planning, reflection pieces, and attendance in the third-grade class. The data also show a difference in patterns of meeting "responsibilities" for each candidate. For example, Brad, until late in the program, did not turn in lesson plans via expected ways, or complete the reflection assignments as expected, requiring additional prompting and support from the supervisor to complete this part of the program requirements. Amy, in contrast, appeared to be absent from the student teaching in unanticipated ways, leading to a range of emails from Denise to Amy to which little or no response was received from Amy. Although Denise continued her supervisory classroom observations of Amy and Brad teaching once a week, few email exchanges were identified in which the candidates informed her about what she would see and how they were working with the mentor teacher. Refer to Table 1 for examples of these data.

What this analysis raised for the program leaders was the question about the nature of the roles and relations between LC1 and LC2 actors in a teaming context. It also raises a challenge for the program (LC1) that teaming contexts may require different approaches to supervising, ones that shift as teacher candidates become members of LC2 and create ways of working together to meet student needs and curricular demands.

Discussion and implications: closings and next steps

In this study, we explored points of contact between a field-based team and university actors, each representing a different languaculture and confronted with frame clashes. These frame clashes were grounded in differing expectations for what should be happening in the classroom or should be displayed by the teacher candidates as meeting the standards and requirements of the program. These frame clashes made visible differences in cultural expectations of the institutionally based actors, clashes that were often bidirectional; that is, the clash had consequences for how actors viewed their work, met their responsibilities, and took up, or not, what others proposed.

This study identified an unanticipated contradiction within the teacher preparation program: While the program's early childhood pedagogy is based on student-centred, culturally relevant, hands-on teaching, and ways of accommodating to diverse needs of children, this model was not visible in the ways in which the program expected candidates to adhere to the Praxis III standards in the field. As indicated in the analysis, the field-based team (re) formulated a rationale for what counted as appropriate ways of planning and lead teaching. However, after providing extensive support for building the team, university expectations returned to the Praxis III model and failed to accommodate to the needs of the team and the mentor teacher. In exploring this lack of accommodation, what the study made visible was the competing standards the team was expected to meet; that is, the state standards for instruction in third grade and standards of the Praxis III that the teachers were to demonstrate to be assessed as competent by the teacher education program.

This study shows the importance of engaging in programmatic research and the need to explore multiple angles of analysis of the nature of the demands and opportunities for different actors at points of contact across institutional boundaries. The unanticipated findings of the impact of competing policies contributed to a decision within the program leadership to shift to a new national approach to assessment of student performance developed by the Teacher Performance Assessment Consortium (TPAC, 2012). This assessment approach involves teacher candidates constructing case studies of children, of student learning, and the analyses of curriculum. This model is more aligned with the program and with the perspective articulated by the mentor teacher in this study. It also supports the reformulation of the role of the supervisor and points to the need for interactions with the candidates and mentor teacher in new ways; areas currently being considered by the program leaders.

Additionally, this study highlights how the roles and relationships among actors need to become a focus for future research, particularly when new, or innovative program designs are being undertaken. For example, Bullough et al. (2002) raised critical questions about mentor teachers' view of teacher candidates' roles in the classroom: Were they simply to turn over the class to the students, fit the students into their curriculum, or support students in engaging in innovative models of team teaching? This latter issue has received little attention in research but is one of the key unanticipated findings of the studies on teaming, as well as our current study.

In this study, we identified bidirectional impacts that need to be addressed, if the field is to meet Zeichner's (2010) call for nonhierarchical relations. Findings also support Darling-Hammond's (2010) argument that researchers on teacher education programs are often faced with unanticipated findings or challenges and ill-defined problems. By grounding our analysis of teaming in an ethnographic perspective, we demonstrated how such findings form anchors or rich points for further analysis both with a single study as well as across studies. Although this study foregrounded the program as a site for inquiry, what it did not include, but the program is considering for the future – given the shift to TPAC, is the development of a research team that includes the mentor teacher and candidates and their questions alongside of the program's questions, creating a dynamic site for inquiry that would include all actors in the research process.

Disclosue statement

No potential conflict of interest was reported by the authors.

References

Agar, M. (2006). Culture: Can you take it anywhere? *International Journal of Qualitative Methods*, 5(2), 1–12. Retrieved from http://www.ualberta.ca/~iiqm/backissues/5_2/PDF/agar.pdf

Agar, M. (2012). Culture: Can you take it anywhere? In L. Monaghan, J. E. Goodman, & J. M. Robinson (Eds.), *A cultural approach to interpersonal communication: Essential readings* (pp. 24). Chichester: John Wiley & Sons.

Anderson-Levitt, K. (Ed.). (2003). *Local meanings, global schooling: Anthropology and world culture theory* (pp. 1–26). New York, NY: Palgrave Macmillan.

Avalos, B. (2011). Teacher professional development in *Teaching and Teacher Education* over ten years. *Teaching and Teacher Education, 27*, 10–20. doi:10.1016/j.tate.2010.08.007

Bates, A. J., Ramirez, L., & Drits, D. (2009). Connecting university supervision and critical reflection: Mentoring and modeling. *The Teacher Educator, 44*(2), 90–112. doi:10.1080/08878730902751993

Beck, C., & Kosnik, C. (2002). Components of a good practicum placement: Student teacher perceptions. *Teacher Education Quarterly, 29*(2), 81–98.

Bloome, D., Carter, S. P., Christian, B. M., Otto, S., & Shuart-Faris, N. (2005). *Discourse analysis & the study of classroom language & literacy events – A microethnographic perspective.* Mahwah, NJ: Lawrence Erlbaum.

Bullough, R. V., & Draper, R. J. (2004). Making sense of a failed triad mentors, university supervisors, and positioning theory. *Journal of Teacher Education, 55*(5), 407–420.

Bullough Jr., R. V., Young, J., Birrell, J. R., Clark, D. C., Egan, M. W., Erickson, L. ... Welling, M. (2002). Teaching with a peer: A comparison of two models of student teacher. *Teaching and Teacher Education, 19*, 57–74. doi:10.1016/S0742-051X(02)00094-X

Cartaut, S., & Bertone, S. (2009). Co-analysis of work in the triadic supervision of preservice teachers based on neo-Vygotskian activity theory: Case study from a French university institute of teacher training. *Teaching and Teacher Education, 25*, 1086–1094. doi:10.1016/j.tate.2009.03.006

Chaliès, S., Bruno-Méard, F., Méard, J., & Bertone, S. (2010). Training preservice teachers rapidly: The need to articulate the training given by university supervisors and cooperating teachers. *Teaching and Teacher Education, 26*, 764–774. doi:10.1016/j.tate.2009.10.012

Cochran-Smith, M., & Lytle, S. L. (2009). *Inquiry as stance.* New York, NY: Teachers College Press.

Cuenca, A., Schmeichel, M., Butler, B. M., Dinkelman, T., & Nichols, J. R. (2011). Creating a "third space" in student teaching: Implications for the university supervisor's status as outsider. *Teaching & Teacher Education, 27*(7), 1068–1077. doi:10.1016/j.tate.2011.05.003

Darling-Hammond, L. (2010). Teacher education and the American future. *Journal of Teacher Education, 61*(1–2), 35–47. doi:10.1177/0022487109348024

Dwyer, C. A. (1994). *Development of the knowledge base for the Praxis III: Classroom performance assessments assessment criteria.* Princeton, NJ: Educational Testing Service.

Edwards, A. (2010). How can Vygotsky and his legacy help us to understand and develop teacher education? In V. Ellis, A. Edwards, & P. Smagorinsky (Eds.), *Cultural-historical perspectives on teacher education and development: Learning teaching* (pp. 63–77). New York, NY: Routledge.

Elstad, E. (2010). University based teacher education in the field of tension between the academic world and practical experience in school: A Norwegian case. *European Journal of Teacher Education, 33*(4), 361–374. doi:10.1080/02619768.2010.504948

Fantozzi, V. (2013). "Oh god, she is looking at every little thing I am doing!" Student teachers' constructions of the observation experience. *Current Issues in Education, 16*(1), 1–13.

Green, J. L., Kelly, G. J., Castamheira, M. L. Esch, J., Frank, C., Hodel, M., Putney, L. & Rodarte, M. (1996). Conceptualizing a basis for understanding: What differences do differences make? *Educational Psychologist, 31* (3–4), 227–234. doi:10.1080/00461520.1996.9653269

Grossman, P., & McDonald, M. (2008). Back to the future: Directions for research in teaching and teacher education. *American Educational Research Journal*, March *45*(1), 184–205. doi:10.3102/0002831207312906

Hamel, C. (2011). Supervision of pre-service teacher: Using internet collaboration tools to support their return to their region of origin. *Canadian Journal of Education, 35*(2), 141–154.

Heath, S. B. (1982). Ethnography in education: Defining the essentials. In P. Gillmore, & A. A. Glatthorn (Eds.), *Children in and out of school: Ethnography and education* (pp. 33–55). Washington, DC: Center for Applied Linguistics.

Ibrahim, A. S. (2013). Approaches to supervision of student teachers in one UAE teacher education program. *Teaching and Teacher Education, 34*, 38–45. doi:10.1016/j.tate.2013.04.002

Isik-Ercan, Z., & Kang, H. Y. (2009, April). Carving a space for themselves: Evolving roles and perspectives in supervising pre-service teachers. Paper presented at the annual meeting of American Educational Research Association, San Diego, CA.

Joram, E. (2007). Clashing epistemologies: Aspiring teachers', practicing teachers', and professors' beliefs about knowledge and research in education. *Teaching and Teacher Education, 23,* 123–135. doi:10.1016/j.tate.2006.04.032

Katz, L., & Green, J. (2012). Exploring continuities and discontinuities for teacher candidates between university and early childhood classrooms. In M.-S. Honig, & S. Neumann (Eds.), *(Doing) Ethnography in early childhood education and care. Proceedings of an international colloquium at the University of Luxembourg.* Luxembourg: University of Luxembourg.

Koerner, M., Rust, F. O., & Baumgartner, F. (2002). Exploring roles in student teaching placements. *Teacher Education Quarterly, 29*(2), 35–58.

LePage, P., Boudreau, S., Maier, S., Robinson, J., & Cox, H. (2001). Exploring the complexities of the relationship between K-12 and college faculty in a nontraditional professional development program. *Teaching and Teacher Education, 17,* 195–211. doi:10.1016/S0742-051X(00)00051-2

Mitchell, J. C. (1984). Typicality and the case study. In R. Ellen (Ed.), *Ethnographic research: A guide to general conduct* (pp. 238–241). New York, NY: Academic Press.

Murray, J., Swennen, A., & Shagrir, L. (2009). Understanding teacher educators' work and identities. In A. Swennen, & M. van der Klink (Eds.), *Becoming a teacher educator: Theory and practice for teacher educators* (pp. 29–44). Dordrecht: Springer.

National Council for Accreditation of Teacher Education. (2010). *Transforming teacher education through clinical practice: A national strategy to prepare effective teachers.* Retrieved June 21, 2012, from http://www.ncate.org/LinkClick.aspx?fileticket=zzeiB1OoqPk%3D&tabid=715

Ochieng' Ong'ondo, C., & Borg, S. (2011). 'We teach plastic lessons to please them': The influence of supervision on the practice of English language student teachers in Kenya. *Language Teaching Research, 15*(4), 509–528. doi:10.1177/1362168811412881

Rorrison, D. (2010). Assessment of the practicum in teacher education: Advocating for the student teacher and questioning the gatekeepers. *Educational Studies, 36*(5), 505–519. doi:10.1080/03055691003729013

Schön, D. (1987). *Educating the reflective practitioner.* San Francisco, CA: Jossey-Bass.

Slick, S. K. (1998). A university supervisor negotiates territory and status. *Journal of Teacher Education, 49*(4), 306–315. doi:10.1177/0022487198049004008

Strike, K. A. (1974). On the expressive potential of behaviorist language. *American Educational Research Journal, 11,* 103–120. doi:10.3102/00028312011002103

Tannen, D. (1979). What's in a frame? Surface evidence for underlying expectations. In R. Freedle (Ed.), *New directions in discourse processing* (pp. 137–181). Norwood, NJ: Ablex.

Teacher Performance Assessment Consortium. (2012). Retrieved July 4, 2013, from www.highered.nysed.gov/pdf/tpac072012.pdf

Wilson, E. K. (2006). The impact of an alternative model of student teacher supervision: Views of the participants. *Teaching and Teacher Education, 22,* 22–31. doi:10.1016/j.tate.2005.07.007

Yusko, B. P. (2004). Caring communities as tools for learner-centered supervision. *Teacher Education Quarterly, 31*(3), 53–72.

Zeichner, K. (2010). Rethinking the connections between campus courses and field experiences in college- and university-based teacher education. *Journal of Teacher Education, 61*(1–2), 89–99. doi:10.1177/0022487109347671

Navigating across academic contexts: Campo and Angolan students in a Brazilian university

Maria Lucia Castanheira[a], Brian V. Street[b] and Gilcinei Teodoro Carvalho[a]

[a]Faculdade de Educação, Universidade Federal de Minas Gerais, Belo Horizonte, Brazil; [b]King's College London, London, United Kingdom

> This paper draws on the Academic Literacies approach to examine tutor/student relations in the production of academic texts. We address issues associated with learning to write in such contexts, through exploring the perspectives of two groups of non-traditional students as they reflect on their experiences in navigating educational contexts in a Brazilian public university. The term non-traditional is used here to refer to students from social groups whose previous generation had no, or very limited, access to university. In order to explore the "hidden features" of the contextualized nature of academic writing, we present two cases: students from Angola and from Campo, both groups not traditionally represented in Brazilian universities. We explored the development of writing in academic contexts by examining tensions identified by these students and their tutors/teachers as they engaged with academic literacies.

Introduction

This paper calls upon the Academic Literacies (AcLits) approach (Lea & Street, 1998) to examine tutor/student relations in the production of academic texts (e.g. research projects, final report or monograph). We address issues associated with learning to write in different university contexts, through exploring non-traditional students' perspectives as they reflect on their experiences in navigating educational contexts; we also examine ways tutors in such programmes viewed aspects of student writing.

In order to explore "hidden features" (Street, 2004, 2009) of the contextualized nature of academic writing, we present two cases: students from Angolan and from Campo (rural Brazil)[1] backgrounds, both not traditionally represented in Brazilian universities. To explore *what counts as* appropriate academic writing in these programmes, we engaged

---

The presence of non-traditional students (e.g. low-income family students, indigenous, *campo* and African students) taking degree and graduate courses in Brazilian universities has increased significantly. Such changes highlight the importance of examining how university tutors and students represent the situated nature of academic writing and the issues involved in navigating across contexts. This paper contributes to the understanding of how these students learn, or learn to negotiate, at least through experience, what counts as academic writing at the university. It demonstrates how teachers' and students' implicit ideologies or epistemologies rise to the surface as indicators writing practices.

in a three-step process. The first step involved interviews of Angolan students and their tutors, focusing on the nature of the feedback afforded them and problems students experienced in writing assignments. The second involved a parallel interview with Campo students, providing a basis from a contrastive analysis of challenges associated with writing (step 3). In addition to the interviews, researchers observed and participated in daily institutional roles with students as teachers, advisors and members of committees from both programmes. Before turning to these analyses, we present a brief discussion of the AcLits perspective guiding these analyses.

Academic Literacies

The AcLits model was developed by Lea and Street (1998), drawing on the theoretical framework of New Literacy Studies (NLS) (Gee, 1990; Street, 1984, 1995). The NLS model recognizes academic writing as social practice within given institutional and disciplinary contexts, and contrasts with dominant skills-based views of writing. In developing this model, Lea and Street conducted an empirical research project in UK universities, where they examined student writing against a background of institutional practices, power relations and identities. Rather than frame their work in terms of "good" and "poor" writing, they suggested that any explanation needed to examine faculty and student expectations around writing to identify what counts as expected or appropriate writing. Findings from their research suggested fundamental gaps between student and faculty understandings of the requirements of student writing, providing evidence at the level of epistemology, authority and contestation over knowledge, rather than at the level of technical skill and surface linguistic competence. Lea and Street explicated three models of student writing, which they termed *study skills, academic socialization* and *academic literacies*. The first model identified was the study skills model that they suggested is based on the assumption that mastery of the correct rules of grammar and syntax, coupled with attention to punctuation and spelling, will ensure student competence in academic writing; it is, therefore, primarily concerned with the surface features of text. In contrast, the second model, academic socialization, assumes students need to be acculturated into the discourses and genres of the institution and that making the features and requirements of these explicit to students will result in their becoming successful writers. The third model, academic literacies, is concerned with meaning-making, identity, power and authority, and foregrounds the institutional nature of what "counts" as knowledge in any particular academic context. It is similar in many ways to the academic socialization model except that it views the processes involved in acquiring appropriate and effective uses of literacy as involving both epistemological levels and social processes, including power relations among people and institutions, and social identities. Lea and Street point out that the models are not presented as mutually exclusive and that each should be seen as encapsulating the other.

The explication of the three models calls for a more in-depth understanding of student writing and its relationship to learning across the academy, thus offering an alternative to deficit models of learning and writing based on autonomous models of literacy (Street, 1984). The AcLits model have been a useful "critical frame" for identifying shortcomings in the current provision at UK universities (Lea & Street, 2006; Lillis, 2006; Lillis & Scott, 2008; Robinson-Pant & Street, 2012; Wingate, 2006, 2008). One implication for pedagogy that is emerging from that body of work is that, unlike genre-based writing pedagogy, writing is understood as learned "implicitly through purposeful participation, not through instruction" (Ivanič, 2004, p. 235). A second implication is that often what counts as "writing" for assessment and evaluation purposes may actually remain "hidden" from students – and in some cases even from their tutors/instructors (Street, 2009). This research, then, has led to a view of the role of teachers as one who provides opportunities for learners to make explicit "hidden" features of academic writing, and to participate in meaningful socially situated literacy events with relevant social goals.

Angolan and Campo students entering a Brazilian university

Both the Angolan and Campo programmes were part of Brazil's policy to have connections with African countries and to extend space in the university to "non-traditional" students. Education is a critical issue in Angola as the country emerges from Civil War and needs teachers to support students at the university level. Similarly, Campo conditions are being subjected to change, making the role of teachers crucial, both at schools and at higher education levels. Therefore, in this paper, we explore the complexities and tensions across contexts and their impact on AcLits as people from Angolan and Campo backgrounds entered a Brazilian university and were required to engage with the expected writing genres and frameworks.

The Angolan students (teachers) came to Brazil in 2012 as masters ($n = 19$) and doctoral students ($n = 9$) in different educational fields (e.g. language, history, psychology, math and science). This educational programme was created as part of a collaborative initiative between Brazilian and African universities to develop educational research on common issues, social inclusion and sustainable development. These postgraduate students spent periods of time at the University in Brazil taking classes and meeting with advisors and back home working on research projects.

The Angola university teachers – who became students in Brazil – had schooling experience during a period of civil war and studied in refugee camps or in local schools in Angola. In the refugee camps, these teachers were required to learn another language (e.g. French) or to attend local schools where they were not permitted to speak their various mother-tongues and had to learn Portuguese. Thus, many of these teachers were multilingual. In contrast, Brazilian university teachers were unfamiliar with some of the languages of the Angolan students. Additionally, Brazilian Portuguese differs in a number of ways from Angolan Portuguese, particularly with regards to the academic register. These differences, therefore, framed the need to examine how the graduate students and their teachers viewed *what counted as* appropriate writing at the postgraduate level and what was involved in producing it.

The Campo students came to the university through policies designed to extend spaces in higher education. Also contributing to their entry were social movements in Brazil that aspire to more places in higher education. The undergraduate students from Campo backgrounds were part of the first-generation students, who finished high school and went to the university. The creation of the Campo (Rural) Pedagogy Program was a university response to demands from what, in Brazil, are termed "landless movements", rural groups that fight for land reform and for access to the land. So, mainly due to shortage of teachers in rural areas, the programme supports agricultural workers, often the sons and daughters of small farmers. Students need to prove social identity as Campo. During the course, students move back and forth between their homeland and the university that is situated in a metropolitan area. After a month at the university, they go back to their area of living and work, where they develop university-related activities with distant tutorial supervision. The language experiences of these students have implications for how they address what is involved in engaging with academic writing.

Methodology

The ethnographic perspective indicated in the AcLits approach encourages researchers to suspend their own models of what is involved with academic writing, and instead to try to find out through observations, interviews and fieldnote-taking what sense participants make of what is going on, in this case their engagement with writing in higher education.

Guided by an ethnographic perspective, Castanheira interviewed students from Angola and their Brazilian tutors about their experience in the programme. She also had the opportunity to have Angolan students in her classes and to discuss initial versions of their research projects. Carvalho likewise worked with undergraduate students from Campo backgrounds and had the opportunity to engage in various activities with them at the university *campus* as well as in the region where they lived while developing research on literacy practices. Street contributed to classes in the university on AcLits and on ethnography that were variously attended by Angolan and Campo students. We developed semi-structured interviews about differences (not difficulties) Angolan students encountered going through the process of becoming students in Brazil and those which Brazilian teachers encountered in advising this group of foreign students. Likewise, Carvalho and Rodrigues interviewed Campo students and made notes about events in which differences between students' and teachers' perspectives on writing arose.

The following analysis examined students' and their teachers' views of *what counted as* appropriate writing at the undergraduate and postgraduate levels. We began by examining how Angolan students described their experience of navigating across academic contexts and interacting with their tutors. The Angolan group's experience was explored as an anchor case for grounding the identification of features of academic writing as seen from their perspectives. So, this anchor case was a resource to build warranted accounts of phenomena from an insider point of view (Green et al., 2011) and was examined in a contrastive analysis with the case of the Campo students. Through this process, we identified differences in the process of writing and advising conducted with both groups of students and their university tutors.

Castanheira interviewed Angolan masters students about the process of writing in Angolan and Brazilian universities, at undergraduate and graduate levels, and Brazilian advisors about the differences in advising Angolan and Brazilian students. Castanheira attempted to minimize the potential power constraints derived from this institutional positioning (interviewer – professor, Brazilian, Portuguese descent, white; interviewees – students, Angolan, black) by conducting interviews with more than one student at once. The students were asked to talk about their university experiences in Angola and Brazil by describing situations that could exemplify differences they identified across university contexts. At the beginning of the interview, the ability of the Angolan students to reflect on the situated nature of academic writing, by comparing differences, was emphasized as an "epistemic privilege" (Mohanty, 1997). This approach was designed to enable them step back from their position as students and to adopt a *metaview*, from which to describe and evaluate their work in this programme. This approach was also adopted with the Brazilian tutors.

Hidden features of AcLits: transcript analysis

The transcripts of the audio records were produced by observing "contextualization cues" to identify the message units (Gumperz, 1985) that were recorded on different lines on the transcript. The Angolan students' and Brazilian tutors' interview transcripts were then examined for descriptions of their experience in working for the first time as academic advisors in the Master Program (cf. Wolcott, 1994). Analysis of these transcripts was then undertaken to identify features of academic literacy that students and teachers had come to recognize as required for writing academic genres.

Guided by the principle of contrastive relevance (Green, Castanheira, Skukauskaite, & Hammond, 2015), a comparative approach to understanding meaning, we examined what was meaningful within a particular social group by contrasting how participants talked about their experience in producing and evaluating AcLits. In turn, this process led to the identification of *rich points* (Agar, 1996) to explore how these different groups of insiders interpreted what they had experienced across educational contexts and the relationships of these aspects with hidden features of academic writing. This process grounded the production of a Matrix Features of Writing across International Academic Contexts (Table 1)

In Table 1, in the first column "cover-term features", we present three groups of features of academic writing: Portuguese language as a contested terrain; positioning; and knowing grammatical Features. In the second and third columns from left to right, we constructed a set of questions to explore what they proposed was going on: *How do we know that the way Brazilians speak in everyday life is not necessarily considered appropriate for academic writing? How should an author position him/herself in academic text? How does the syntax of Brazilian Portuguese work in an academic text? What kind of writing problem do these students have?* As indicated in Table 1, students and tutors were puzzled by similar aspects; however, they seemed to have very different views of what was going on. In the following sections, we analyse the implications of these different perspectives for understanding what counted as AcLits. The differences are presented as sources of tension that were consequential in understanding the dimensions of academic literacy. Given the scope of this paper, we will focus our discussion on aspects related to Portuguese language as a contested terrain and positioning.

Portuguese language as a contested terrain

The first feature that became visible through the analysis of the interviews was that Portuguese language had become a contested terrain for participants. That is, although Brazilians and Angolans use Portuguese, in practice the varieties used differ considerably leading to a constant need to negotiate syntactic forms and lexical choices. This raises the sociolinguistic question of the relationship between how different Brazilian social groups and Angolans speak in everyday life and what is considered appropriate in academic writing in the Brazilian context – an issue that also arises in academic contexts internationally as students move from everyday life situations to academic contexts (Lea & Street, 1998).

Table 1. Features of writing across International Academic Contexts – matrix grounded in interviews with Angolan students and Brazilian tutors.

Cover-term features	Students' point of view	Tutors' point of view
(1) Portuguese language as a contested terrain	*How do we know that the way Brazilians speak in everyday life is not necessarily considered appropriate for academic writing?* • Distinction between formal and informal register and linguistic variation [e.g. uses of personal pronouns] • Local meaning for words [e.g. Lavra (Mining in Brazilian Portuguese; Tillage, in Angola Portuguese), meter (In Brazil, the word *meter* can have a sexual connotation as in *stick*)] • Local meaning for idiomatic expressions • For someone that is not working with the literature/they are going to think that it [informal register or dialect markers] is normal/even in an academic text	*Which language are students using?* • Distinction between Portuguese language and unknown dialects • Inadequate use of words (e.g. "meter" – *stick*) • Tension: different Portuguese(s) (e.g. from Brazil, Portugal and Angola)
(2) Positioning	*How an author should position him/herself in academic text?* • Critiques about having a "critical discourse" in the research project • Writing within a discipline or approach • One should not reveal his/her position in the text • Uses of and reasons for I or we	*Why is it so difficult for these students to be clear about their position as author in their text?* • Students are not used to making contrasts between various text • Some students are afraid to take political positions • The only experience in writing was from an statistical perspective
(3) Knowing grammatical features	*How does the syntaxes of Brazilian Portuguese work in an academic text?* • All of us know/that "a predicate" is central piece in a phrase • But I understand that/[we need to learn] writing academic texts/adapted to the logic of Brazilian academic Portuguese	*What kind of writing problem do these students have?* • They don't know how to write as a general evaluation position among tutors • Problems identified: text structure/ from paragraph organization problems/to legibility of the text/citations problem/

Reflecting on the process of becoming a student in a Brazilian university, Angolan students pointed out the impact of being immersed in what they called a "Brazilian linguistic market". For them, this involved the challenge of understanding the "many Brazils" (or ways of speaking Portuguese in Brazil) and its relation to conversation in the university and in writing.

INTERDISCIPLINARY AND INTERCULTURAL PROGRAMMES

Transcript 1. "Brazilian linguistic market".

Silvio
1. we got here
2. and we found many Brazils
3. in terms of Portuguese language
4. that is not easy
5. for an Angolan
6. for a Mozambiquean
7. for a Portuguese
8. ahn
9. I was saying to my colleagues
10. it is easier for a francophone
11. to adapt to Brazilian Portuguese
12. he is going to learn with Brazilians
13. and we
14. from a Portuguese speaking country
15. we bring the language
16. we think that we speak the same language
17. and we get "distracted" often
18. in elaborating an academic text
19. the person needs to know
20. how does the syntax of Brazilian Portuguese works
21. and they will have other difficulties
22. in my case
23. the problem of [distinguishing] formal and informal Portuguese
24. both of them are circulating
25. in the Brazilian linguistic market
26. the person has no idea which one is **the** Portuguese
27. for someone that is not working with the [actual Brazilian academic] literature
28. they will think that it is normal
29. even in an academic text
30. to write "ocê" instead of você

In Transcript 1, Silvio provides elements for understanding his and his colleagues' experiences in the "Brazilian linguistic market". In lines 1–7, Silvio positions himself and others that come from Portuguese-speaking countries other than Brazil on separate grounds, emphasizing his view that coming from one side or the other provides a very distinct experience and knowledge of what it means to speak Portuguese. From his point of view, the very knowledge of Portuguese that people like him already have may bring difficulties for understanding and using of Brazilian Portuguese (lines 8–18): for instance, to "bring the language, [to] think that we speak the language" makes them get "distracted". The use of "distracted" in this context indicates that such people often find themselves engaged in a conversation or in writing but not paying attention to what language features can potentially bring misunderstandings among the parties involved in the situation.

In lines 18–29, Silvio provides some examples of the features from which they get "distracted" and that require other kind of effort on their part. One of them is the need to be aware that the syntax of Brazilian Portuguese differs from other Portuguese[s] when writing a text, and the other, the need to distinguish the differences between formal and informal Brazilian Portuguese and how and when they "apply" in the academic context. As also indicated by the emphasis in *the* (line 25) and the reference to *the literature* (line 26), implying academic literature published in Brazilian Portuguese, Silvio is conscious of what is involved in engaging with "academic" registers of Portuguese, showing understanding that they differ from those of everyday life usage as well as from the academic registers used in Angola.

Another student, Ildeu, also commented on how, as students, he and colleagues from Angola used to refer to their teachers as Mr and Mrs, and their surprise at the reaction of Brazilian teachers in insisting they be called *você* (you) and by their first names, indicating that there were also cultural differences in the ways relationship between teacher and students is portrayed and addressed across university contexts. A key issue that the data raised is how the contextualized nature of language use affects the academic experience of students, often in contrast with their previous knowledge of and competence of a particular language.

It is interesting to note that in explaining the situation he found himself in after arriving in Brazil, Silvio draws on Bourdieu's sociological framework to refer to Brazilian *linguistic market* (line 24). Here we can see how he is exploring theories contemplated on theories of language and education to analyse his social and institutional experiences as well as to position himself as one that already belongs to the academic world.

Tutors also provided observations that led to understanding Portuguese language as contested terrain. Claudia, a tutor and researcher of history of education, talked about what she learned reading transcripts produced by one of her students. Her student had been to Angola and interviewed people from there and, according to Claudia, she "transcribed it *exactly* in the language from there". Claudia suggested that it was only when she looked at the transcripts produced by her student that she was able to see the extent in which Portuguese spoken in Angola is different from that spoken by Brazilians. However, she was still not quite sure on how to describe and talk about these differences. After observing that her student "speaks Portuguese well", she stated: "but it is obvious/ she incorporates *lots* of things/ I forgot the dialect they speak there/ she says things such as/ meter (stick)". Like the students, Claudia is troubled by these differences. From her point of view, these may be originated by the "incorporation" of elements of a dialect that she did not know, and the evidence of this was the use of words such as "meter", which has different connotations across contexts and which is not appropriate in a Brazilian academic context.

Both students and tutors identified Portuguese language as a contested terrain; each of them took a different perspective on this matter. One aspect here that may be of considerable significance, for the study of AcLits in international contexts, is the complex metacommentary that Silvio brought to bear on this situation. If we recognize that students described as "not able to write" may in fact, like Silvio, have considerable understanding of the linguistic and social processes involved in moving into academic genres, then the approach might be re-balanced away from the dominant model of students as "ignorant" to a more balanced and complex interactive view taking account of the different perspectives involved in such situations.

It was this more complex overview that we attempted to develop here as we worked with students and their tutors from different linguistic and cultural backgrounds. Like Claudia, many tutors work in different fields in which language is not a focus of study (e.g. history, psychology, natural sciences). That also raises a question of how an understanding of language differences and its use across contexts can be addressed with tutors from different backgrounds. Given that Claudia and her colleagues moved on and supported their students in accomplishing their goals (all masters students successfully defended their thesis), future studies are needed to examine if, and how, an initial negative perspective on students' language from the part of tutors can be redefined.

Positioning

Another feature identified by students and tutors as relevant in writing academic text was that of positioning (Table 1), as they reflected on whether or how an author should present his or her point of view, use first- or third-person pronouns or take a political position. Analysis of conversations around this feature of academic writing demonstrated various nuances. During the interviews, this theme came up when a masters student, Ildeu, commented that one of the corrections he received in his research project was because he was "not using the first voice of discourse". However, he said that this critique was not consistent with recommendations he read in different texts. According to him, he found that "some authors/ they point out that the author should not use the first voice in the text/ always to approach the text/ as if you were not there". Silvio, on the other hand, revealed that he had already made a decision on this matter. As he explained: "In my project/ I elected to always/ write the text in the first person plural/ given the contribution of so many people/ that are implied in this use/ and that without their presence/ the collaboration of these people/ the research would have found many obstacles/ this is a way of saying thanks to these people".

It is important to note the ways students were searching for, questioning and proposing reasons that would ground their decisions about using *I* or *We* in their texts. Moreover, it is important to note that their considerations pointed to different views of science and different relationships that an author can establish with others in the process of science construction. For Ildeu, the avoidance of use of *I/We* was necessary to observe a particular view of science as neutral and objective, for Silvio, the use of *We* pointed to a view of science as the result of an effort made by many individuals. Silvio felt comfortable with this decision of "always" using *We*, without yet realizing that very soon he could be called to differentiate his own position from other authors that he explored in his current research. It is clear, then, that there is a need to understand that the use of *I* or *We* in an academic text is not simply a matter of one or the other but a matter of understanding the different "alliances" that can be made as one weaves his/her position in a text.

We see here what has been referred to in the literature as "voice" (Street, 2009). Silvio indicates that an academic view of "voice" is different from his own assumptions about how to indicate position and person and he points to his use of "we" as a way of acknowledging the support and collaboration of others. However, such choice was neither explicit in his writing nor assured him a "safe" and "correct" usage of the pronoun "we" as an author of an academic text or as a researcher in a particular field, given that the (re)presentation of an author's voice in an academic text involves a weaving of "positionings" expressed in various ways (e.g. as a single person – masters student, a researcher; or as a person that belongs to different groups – e.g. a group of teachers or a group of researchers on language and education).

Silvio added another nuance, related to author's positioning in a text, when he commented on the fact that he was learning about ethnography. He remembered that the research methodology tutor called his attention to the aspect of taking a *critical* position in his text. When Castanheira asked if it was because he was critical and he should not be, Silvio explained: "[it was] a lack of thought on my side/ this is because I began to do an ethnography/ isn't it/ a research from an ethnographic perspective/ and in this perspective/ the ethnographer/ doesn't judge the facts/ he only describes and presents from a scientific view/ sometimes when I am writing/ I talk too much/ I reveal my perspective." Ildeu complemented this in saying that advisors pointed out that students very often adopted an "ought to" position: for example, "everything is wrong, the State has to do X and Y, the teachers have to do X and Y". The students asked themselves: "*Why* the advisors say this? There is no space for political position in an academic text?" Remembering that Angolan students have a history of political engagement to transform and improve the social and educational conditions of their country, after a long period of civil war, can help the advisor to understand why they adopted an "ought to" position, as noticed by their advisors. However, students struggled to find space for this sort of commitment in an academic text, particularly when it seemed to clash with a particular research approach they were learning (e.g. ethnography).

From the point of view of tutors, students' political perspectives and affiliation to particular research approach could also be a source of difficulties in writing academic texts. While many students were called to attend to how they were being critical, Claudia referred to the problem, as she saw it. As she said, one of her students was initially *less* prepared to be "political" than was acceptable in the Brazilian context. She remembered that when her advisee arrived in Brazil she was "very much afraid of the risk of taking some political positions." As she explained: "she used to be more afraid than she is now [two years later]/ I saw her saying things/ very open/ *the [Angolan] government is deceiving the people*". Claudia's comments can be better understood if we take into account what she referred to as her student's moral and religious affiliation as well as preoccupation with being critical of a government that was funding their graduate studies. Marlene, another tutor of the Angolan students, on the other hand, emphasized that students had only the "experience of writing a monograph". According to her, "they organize the text and it has introduction/ development and conclusion" but they had very little experience in confronting different texts, finding out what authors have to say and taking a position.

Contrasting students' and tutors' considerations on the matter of what was involved in how they presented self and took positions in an academic text demonstrated the variety of factors that come into play. The issue of how students write in such a way that their position is evident but at the same time adheres to the particular genre requirements of the discipline, such as whether to make their political position explicit, is familiar from many contexts and we illustrated here how it is expressed in this particular context. For instance, at the end of an interview, Ildeu felt compelled to make the following comment: Emphasizing that what he was going to say was something that he "felt deep inside", Ildeu offered another way of seeing how going through this particular academic development programme provoked changes in his ways of seeing and understanding the function of the university, the diploma, science and knowledge science production. In this case, we argue that this epistemological shift was provoked by how he was challenged to become an "author of science" and "not to be the subject of science". As he says, "to do something" was an appeal that resonated with the political engagement of Angolan students in reconstructing their country after a long period of war. So, he may now seize on being an author of science as a way of "doing something" that enables him to put himself in the text in a way that fits with this political perspective and at the same time with the academic genres he is expected to conform with.

What we learned from contrasting students' and tutors' perspectives interviews of the kind described above was that students were struggling with a broad and varied range of concerns and we had here drawn attention to the following: "denaturalizing" personal/ social language knowledge and experience; dealing with the need to find the proper way to position themselves as authors of a text and of science (e.g. position and voice); redefining the understanding of what counts as "scientific" production and the student's role in this process. We would add from the AcLits perspective that these features of academic writing need to be explicitly addressed by both tutors and students – a key issue for future work in this field.

INTERDISCIPLINARY AND INTERCULTURAL PROGRAMMES

Extending the analysis to Campo

In previous sections, we examined how Angolan students' and their tutors' experience enabled us to describe and evaluate different features of academic writing, particularly those related to *Portuguese language as a contested terrain* and *positioning*. We move now to the examination of how, and if, similar issues emerged and were addressed in the context of a Campo undergraduate course.

The encounter, and use of academic terms, was also a feature of university life pointed out by Campo students, as we can see in the following segments of interviews (Transcripts 2–4) conducted by Carvalho and Rodrigues.

Transcript 2.   Positioning in science.

Ildeu:
1. I should confess
2. and I say this because it is what I feel deep inside
3. our way of seeing the scientific life has changed a lot
4. I used to think that the grad school is an institution
5. where the individual went to get his diploma
6. and get on with his life
7. I now believe that being here at [institution name] particularly here in this [department's name] showed me that things are not exactly like that
8. here the person is call upon to be the author of science
9. and not to be the subject of science
10. you are called to produce and so on
11. to do some thing

Transcript 3.   Learning new words.

Maria
1. we learn many new words
2. the way teachers speak
3. we pick that up
4. there are always new words that
5. mark a semester
6. for example
7. dialectic

Transcript 4.   Learning new words.

André
1. I was already homesick for these words
2. Dichotomy
3. Paradigm

Maria (Transcript 3), a student from a rural background, highlighted that each semester they learned many new words in the university context and that there was always a word that marks a semester (e.g. dialectic). She also pointed out that teachers had a different way of speaking and that students came to pick that up. Maria's comments showed her awareness that the ways she encountered and used language previously were different from what she came to know in the university context, and she implied that the sustained immersion in this context could lead students to become a little like those teachers they met. These differences were also indicated by Andre, another student from a rural background (Transcript 4). He said that when he spent a period at home, in a rural region, he was "homesick" for the words he had learned in the university context (e.g. paradigm, dichotomy). Andre's comments helped us see how affect or emotion may be tied to the process of acquiring new identities associated with ways of speaking as one enters a new academic space. Luiza's comment (Transcript 5) added a different nuance to this reflection. Coming from a socially and linguistically stigmatized group (rural origins), Luiza reproduced the discourse that gives differential social value to rural or urban ways of speaking, and what is "urban" here was represented by the university teachers' way of speaking. As her rather ironic use of "chic" may suggest, the university way of speaking was seen as a practice associated with an urban upper class lifestyle.

Through these examples, we saw a socialization issue involving how students come to belong to the new context of "university" – but academic socialization does not fully capture this issue as the power relations and the cultural differences also need addressing. The AcLits approach focuses in addition, then, on how such students learned to use new words and took on board a new identity. When students returned to their Campo background, they did not encounter these words, so they felt "homesick" for the university words. They experienced a different vision of the world; the words were more than mere lexical items but in fact signified deeper identity and power relationships. In these examples, the students signalled that the repertoire they learned at university may provide them with a new and different identity – in this case as a "university student" – but they also represented the use of words such as "paradigm" as indicating that they were becoming "chic", a more parodic and less hierarchical way of describing it. Their ability to use these ways of speaking involved recognition of the role of language and words as part of a larger power game. Again tutors and researchers needed to recognize how students are able to make metacommentaries on *what is going on*, to bring linguistic and social comment to bear as in Luiza's reference to the "urban" context but also her parody of the dominant terms by describing her use of them as "chic".

As with the Angolan students, the issue of political voice and position was also raised. The Campo students likewise asked if there was "No place for a political position in project or academic writing in general?" Much university writing is expected to move beyond a "personal" perspective and to provide a more detached view. This is particularly evident at a later stage of students' university education, when they are finishing their degree. For instance, Lucas, a Campo student, who had learned the surface features of such writing, still came up against the political dimension of engagement with challenging ideas and some of the contradictions involved in explicit as opposed to implicit writing, as we will demonstrate below. So although the formal advice is "be explicit", in fact, students were not expected to express their political engagement explicitly. In a final paper, Lucas, who had interviewed subjects and filled out a form about their reading practices, wrote to one of his respondents:

> I am happy with the results because they show their interest in reading and I believe that it is a good start. I see that the sons and daughters of proletariat have a thirst for understanding what they read and all the complexity behind it.

Someone from his committee picked this up and agreed with it but advised the student not to use this way of expressing the point, such as the explicit sentiment "I am happy". In one of his interviews, Lucas argued back against this criticism, as we can see in Transcript 6.

Transcript 5.   Learning new words.

Luiza
1. a new word that I remembered I learned here was
2. proficient reader
3. it's very chic
4. isn't it?

Transcript 6.   Affirming political position.

Lucas
1. I think the academy is not ready for a critique like this
2. in the sense
3. in the sense of struggle
4. of emphasis on ideology
5. the major difficulty I had was related to this
6. the political aspect of my text
7. my political ideology of expressing myself
8. in the text
9. it was my political choice to position myself in the text
10. I think this caused me trouble because the academy is not ready for this

From Lucas' perspective, the critique about the way he expressed his feelings in a final paper was related to the fact that the "academy is not prepared" for the kind of political positioning he expressed in his texts. As he made clear, it was his choice to emphasize his political ideology and that this choice itself was also understood as a political one.

Conclusions

A question that arose with respect to both Angolan students and those from Campo backgrounds was, "How do we know why the way in which Brazilians speak in everyday life is not necessarily considered appropriate for academic writing?" This is, we argue, a similar issue to that associated with academic registers in other languages – much of the AcLits research, whether in UK English (Lea & Street, 1998; Lillis, 2006; Robinson-Pant & Street, 2012), US English (Prior, 1998; Russell, 1991), French (Delcambre & Lahanier, 2013), brings out the ways in which academic registers and genres differ from those of everyday usage in ways that many students find confusing and that lead to the problems with academic writing that constantly concern university staff. This research also indicates that there is not one, uniform "academic register" in any of these languages – rather the writing requirements vary with discipline, year of study and level of programme (Lea & Street, 1998; Scott & Lillis, 2008; Thesen & van Pletzen, 2006). The university, then, is not a homogenous environment but rather involves a complex range of writing requirements at different levels of course development and in different disciplines. The pedagogic question that arises from this finding is how far the university will go to offer students support in recognizing, reflecting and acquiring these different genres. To address this question, we argue that it is also important to recognize that students themselves have views on what is going on and are able to draw upon conceptual and analytic resources to explain the "problems", again. Therefore, this finding suggests that a key step for tutors involves recognizing this student awareness, and to build on it, in order to develop their AcLits.

The analysis presented in this paper made visible various features of students' academic life experience and awareness as they navigated across schooling contexts (e.g. across countries and across levels of schooling). Students offered ways of understanding that what counts as Portuguese language, for instance, was locally defined and context dependent (e.g. Brazilian linguistic market is different from Angola linguistic market; Portuguese varieties spoken in Brazilian rural and urban areas are seen and valued differently). From this perspective, the analysis showed that students experience Portuguese language as a contested terrain. On the other hand, the analysis also provided evidence that knowledge and use of academic language (written or spoken) will differ from varieties and ways of speaking experienced by students in non-academic contexts. Heath (1983) has already provided evidence of implications of home/ school differences in her account of "ways with words", and her recent book that extends her previous work, entitled up *Words at Work and Play* (Heath, 2012). In the present context, we argue that such an account applies not only to students from different "class" and "ethnic" backgrounds but also to more "traditional" students from higher classes, who are normally assumed to make a seamless transition to university. In fact, *all* students encounter difficulties in learning the new academic genres required at university, although their experience may differ according to their previous backgrounds.

In this paper, we took account of developments in Brazil in the last decade in terms of access for students from diverse sociocultural backgrounds to higher education and linked this to theoretical work addressing similar experiences evident in international contexts. In particular, we drew on the AcLits approach to writing practices in higher education and adopted an ethnographic perspective in attempting to address participants' own views of *what is going on*. We have focused on linguistic and textual features signalled as key in academic discourse production by those engaged in the writing process in a Brazilian university, such as discourse features and positioning. We made use of various sources of data: supervisor's feedback to students; interviews with students about the feedback they received from their supervisors; and interviews with supervisors about the challenges they face in this process of supporting students in their academic writing. In this changing educational context, we identified some familiar and some new elements in the long-standing challenge to both students and university faculty. The meta awareness by students themselves of the linguistic and social features of their encounter with the university represented evidence of a development of some of the earlier insights in the field with particular reference to the complex social and ethnic contexts in a Brazilian university described here (cf. Rodrigues, 2012; Ferreira, 2013; Vieira, 2014).

The results of the analyses presented here, then, highlighted the importance of examining how university tutors help students to understand the situated nature of academic writing, and we have recognized the importance that such engagement with literacy is a social practice, not just a technical skill and the value of adopting an ethnographic perspective, rather than just measuring and evaluating outcomes from a distance.

Note

1. The terms *Campo* and *Rural* in a broad sense can refer to people who work and live in rural areas. However, locally, given the history of social movements for agrarian reform in Brazil, the word Campo often is used to refer to people who see themselves as more politically active in such social movements.

References

Agar, M. (1996). *The professional stranger: An informal introduction to ethnography* (2nd ed.). New York, NY: Academic Press.

Delcambre, I., & Lahanier, D. (Eds.) (2013). *International studies on writing at the university: comparisons and evolutions*. (Perspectives on Writing Series). New York, NY: Reuter.

Ferreira, M. L. S. (2013). *Letramentos acadêmicos em contexto de expansão do ensino superior no Brasil* (Doctoral dissertation). Universidade Federal de Minas Gerais, Belo Horizonte, Brazil.

Gee, J. P. (1990). *Social linguistics and literacies: Ideology in discourse*. London: Falmer Press.

Green, J. L. (2011). Ethnography as epistemology: An introduction to educational ethnography. In J. Arthur, M. I. Waring, R. Coe, & L. V. Hedges, (Eds.), *Research methodologies and methods in education*. London: Sage.

Green, J. L., Castanheira, M. L., Skukauskaite, A., & Hammond, J. (2015). Developing a multi-faceted research process: An ethnographic perspective for reading across traditions. In N. Markee (Ed.), *Handbook of classroom discourse and interaction*. Hoboken, NJ: Wiley.

Gumperz, J. (1985). Interactional sociolinguistics in the study of schooling. In J. Cook Gumperz (Ed.), *The social construction of literacy* (pp. 50–75). Cambridge: Cambridge University Press.

Heath, S. B. (1983). *Ways with words*. Cambridge: Cambridge University Press.

Heath, S. B. (2012). *Words at work and play: Three decades in family and community life*. Cambridge: Cambridge University Press.

Ivanič, R. (2004). Discourses of writing and learning to write. *Language and Education, 18*(3), 220–245. doi:10.1080/09500780408666877

Lea, M. R., & Street, B. (1999). Writing as academic literacies: understanding textual practices in higher education. In C. N. Candlin & K. Hyland (Eds.), *Writing: Texts, processes and practices* (pp. 62–81). London: Longman.

Lea, M. R., & Street, B. V. (1998). Student writing in higher education: An academic literacies approach. *Studies in Higher Education, 23*(2), 157–172. doi:10.1080/03075079812331380364

Lea, M. R., & Street, B. V. (2006). The 'academic literacies' model: Theory and applications. *Theory into Practice, 45*, 368–377. doi:10.1207/s15430421tip4504_11

Lillis, T. (2006). Moving towards an academic literacies pedagogy: Dialogues of participation. In L. Ganobcsik-Williams (Ed.), *Teaching academic writing in UK. Higher education: Theories, practices and models* (pp. 30–45). London: Palgrave Macmillan.

Lillis, T., & Scott, M. (2008). Defining academic literacies research: Issues of epistemology, ideology and strategy. *Journal of Applied Linguistics, 4*, 5–32. doi:10.1558/japl.v4i1.5

Mohanty, S. P. (1997). *Literary theory and the claims of history: Postmodernism, objectivity, multicultural politics*. Ithaca, NY: Cornell University Press.

Prior, P. (1998). *Writing/disciplinarity: A sociohistoric account of literate activity in the academy*. Mahwah, NJ: Lawrence Erlbaum Associates.

Robinson-Pant, A., & Street, B. (2012). 'Students' and tutors' understanding of 'new' academic literacy practices. In M. Castelló & C. Donahue (Eds.), *University writing: Selves and texts in academic societies*. Bingley: Emerald Press.

Rodrigues, A. P. (2012). *Escrita acadêmica em contexto de formação de professores do Campo* (Master's thesis). School of Education, Universidade Federal de Minas Gerais, Belo Horizonte.

Russell, D. (1991). *Writing in the academic disciplines, 1870–1990: A curricular history*. Carbondale: South Illinois University Press.

Street, B. (1995). *Social literacies*. London: Longman.

Street, B. (2009). 'Hidden' features of academic paper writing. *Working Papers in Educational Linguistics*, UPenn 24(1), 1–17.

Street, B. V. (1984). *Literacy in theory and practice*. Cambridge: Cambridge University Press.

Street, B. V. (1996). Academic literacies. In D. Baker, J. Clay, & C. Fox (Eds.), *Alternative ways of knowing: Literacies, numeracies* (pp. 101–134). London: Falmer Press.

Street, B. V. (2004). Academic literacies and the 'new orders': Implications for research and practice in student writing in HE. *LATISS: Learning and Teaching in the Social Sciences*, 1, 9–20. doi:10.1386/ltss.1.1.9/0

Thesen, L., & van Pletzen, E. (Eds.). (2006). *Academic literacy and the languages of change*. London: Continuum.

Vieira, E. A. P. (2014). *Letramento Acadêmicos: (Re) Significações e (Re)Posicionamentos de Sujeitos Discursivos* (Doctoral dissertation). Instituto de Estudos da Linguagem, UNICAMP, São Paulo.

Wingate, U. (2006). Doing away with study skills. *Teaching in Higher Education*, 11(4), 457–469. doi:10.1080/13562510600874268

Wingate, U. (2008). Enhancing students' transition to university through online pre-induction courses. In R. Donnelly & F. Mc Sweeney (Eds.), *Applied eLearning and eTeaching in higher education* (pp. 178–200). Hershey, PA: Information Science Reference, IGI Global.

Wolcott, H. (1994). *Transforming qualitative data: Description, analysis and interpretation*. CA: Sage.

Interdisciplinary dialogues as a site for reflexive exploration of conceptual understandings of teaching–learning relationships

Judith L. Green[a], Yun Dai[a], Jenna Joo[a], Edward Williams[a], Ang Liu[b] and Stephen C.-Y. Lu[b]

[a]Education, Gevirtz Graduate School of Education, University of California, Santa Barbara, CA, USA; [b]Viterbi School of Engineering, University of Southern California, Los Angeles, CA, USA

> This study examines what the members of an interdisciplinary research alliance, at the intersection of Engineering and Education Ethnography, learned through ongoing dialogues among members (2012–2014). The analyses make visible how, and for what purpose(s), this interdisciplinary *research alliance* was constructed, including the theoretical/conceptual roots of perspectives guiding the members of the alliance, and how these orienting perspectives served as anchors for exploring points where differences in understandings became visible to members. By tracing responses that members had to differences in understandings, we examine how the differences became resources for members to (re)examine their initial assumptions and understandings of particular teaching–learning processes, and how these differences supported members, individually and collectively, in extending and (re)formulating their understandings of the relationship between and among teaching and learning processes that constituted *no distance education* processes. Through the presentation of three *telling cases*, we make visible how the dialogues led to different levels of ethnographic analysis (cases 1 and 2). Each was undertaken to develop an understanding of what counted as the *no distance education* process, both at the design and institutional level across national institutions as well as in the course across times and events. The third telling case explores transformations in understanding particular aspects of teaching–learning relationships that the members reported were related to the ongoing dialogues and ethnographic research.

Introduction

Today, nationally and internationally, calls are emerging for examining how, why and under what conditions researchers develop particular inter-transdisciplinary projects and for examining what is learned through such projects. At the centre of such calls are two different goals for such alliances – problem solving and developing fundamental understanding of complex phenomena (e.g. Swiss Academy of Arts and Sciences, 2014; US National Academies of Sciences, Engineering & Institutes of Medicine, 2004). This use of "phenomena" and "explore" twice needs some revision. Underlying these calls is recognition that what counts as fundamental understandings of a phenomenon often emerges as participants within an interdisciplinary collaboration pose questions and explore the developing discourse of the group.[1]

In this study, we explore how dialogic work among members of an interdisciplinary research alliance, at the intersection of engineering and educational ethnography (Castanheira, Crawford, Green & Dixon, 2000), created a series of (un)anticipated opportunities for members to (re)examine fundamental conceptual and epistemological perspectives about both the nature of, and ways of studying, teaching–learning relationships and design principles guiding what Professor Stephen Lu (SCLU),[2] called a *no distance education* (NDE) approach. At the centre of this study was a general education course entitled the *Principles and Practices of Global Innovation*, the initial offering with a global initiative he called the iPodia Alliance (http://ipodia.usc.edu/partnership/partners/).

The analyses of what members learned through ongoing dialogues are presented in three parts. In part 1, we examine email chains and meetings that initiated the research alliance's exploration of how, and for what purpose(s), this interdisciplinary *research alliance* was constructed. In part 2, we present a series of theoretical concepts guiding analyses of particular events that served as anchors for exploring points where differences in understandings became visible to members. By tracing responses of members to differences in understandings, we examine how these differences became a resource for members to (re)examine their initial assumptions and understandings of particular teaching–learning processes. In part 3, we present a series of *telling cases* (Mitchell, 1984), each focusing on a particular interactional ethnographic analysis. Case 1 examines the complex set of actors involved in designing, implementing and participating in the "no distance education". Case 2 examines the structuring processes and course activity across 20 weeks in order to identify what counted (Heap, 1991) as NDE. Case 3 explores points where differences in understanding of the nature of teaching–learning processes led to transdisciplinary (re)consideration of particular conceptual perspectives.

Guiding questions and conceptual approach

Two questions guided the analysis of the reflexive processes undertaken.

- Why, how, in what ways, and for what purposes did the engineering professor/designer and his team engage in dialogues with the interactional ethnographic team?
- What layers of analyses were necessary to explore unanticipated challenges faced by alliance members in developing mutual understandings of what was happening as the instructor engaged the interdisciplinary and globally based undergraduate students in learning the principles of design thinking for global innovation?

These questions, as indicated previously, framed an iterative, recursive and abductive reflexive process (e.g. Agar, 2006; Green, Skukauskaite, & Baker, 2012) undertaken to uncover the conceptual understandings of particular members as well as instructional decisions of the engineering professor as he designed, and then engaged students in, opportunities for learning design thinking processes and practices for global innovation projects (c.f., Jing & Lu, 2010; Lu, 2008).

Framing the reflexive processes

In this section, we present a series of conceptual arguments that constitute the *logic-in-use* (Birdwhistell, 1977) guiding the different analyses undertaken: *stepping back from ethnocentrism, languaculture, rich points, telling cases* and *intertextuality as a social accomplishment*. Rather than presenting each conceptual argument in turn, we present them in relationship to analyses undertaken. For each analysis, we present the theoretical/conceptual arguments guiding this logic-in-use, and how this logic-in-use led to the construction of particular data sets from the archived records (e.g. email exchanges, video recordings, web resources for students, web descriptions of the course and fieldnotes of meetings) necessary for exploring what was interactionally accomplished in the dialogues among alliance members as well as between the instructor and students in the course.

By tracing recurrent references to particular challenges, understandings and actions across intertextually tied (Bloome & Egan-Robertson, 1993) texts (e.g. emails, dialogues, videos and web-based materials), we uncover ways in which members made visible changes in their conceptual understandings of teaching–learning relationship. Underlying this approach is the following conceptual argument by Lima (1995) who, drawing on conceptual work of Vygotsky, Wallon and Freire, framed the need to explore individual-collective relationships when seeking to understand what is being discursively developed at both the collective and individual levels:

> We have two dimensions of development: one that resides in the individual and the other in the collectivity. Both are interdependent and create each other. Historically created possibilities of cultural development are themselves transformed by the processes through which individuals acquire the cultural tools that are or become available in their context. (p. 447–448)

This conceptual argument frames how we understand the ways in which discourse became a resource for the alliance and points to the need to trace backward and forward in time the intertextual roots and routes (pathways) leading to, and from, particular observed/inscribed *rich points* (Agar, 2006), where differences in understandings were identified. This, and related conceptual arguments, guided multiple layers and angles of analysis necessary for constructing *warranted claims* (Heap, 1995; Strike, 1989) about how what was accomplished, at a particular point in time, or activity among participants, was consequential for what was constructed and/or understood in subsequent times and events in both the course and the dialogues among alliance members.

Part 1: Stepping back from ethnocentrism – uncovering the origins of the research alliance

The first guiding principle of the logic-in-use, *stepping back from ethnocentrism,* was proposed by Heath (1982), who argued that "Fieldworkers should attempt to uphold the ideal of leaving aside ethnocentrism and maintaining open acceptance of the behaviours (actions) of all members of the group being studied" (p. 35). Building on this argument, Green et al. (2012) proposed a series of actions that ethnographers can take to analysis of what constitutes emic, or insider, chains of discourse (oral and written) that alliance members used to signal intertextual ties among past present and future texts (email, spoken, graphic, other). These conceptual arguments provide theoretical rationale for why ethnographers seek insider or emic understandings of ways of perceiving, acting, interpreting and understanding what members of a sustaining social group are dialogically accomplishing (Heath, 1982). From this perspective, members of such groups, through their discourse and actions,

- Propose, orient to, acknowledge and recognize what counts as socially (academically, institutionally and/or personally) significant within and across times and events;
- Jointly (discursively) construct and name (reference) actions and events;

- Construct norms and expectations, roles and relationships, and rights and obligations within and across events, times and actors;
- Draw on past events, references and understandings in a developing event;
- Make visible to the ethnographer (or other members), at points of emic-etic (insider–outsider) tensions, what counts as expected, anticipated or negotiated actions and meanings. (Adapted from Green et al., 2012, Table 39.2, p. 39)

Viewing the group's actions and discourse from this perspective provided a lens for our analysis team to step back from what we had experienced in the moments of dialogue and virtual observations of the course. By identifying and analysing the dialogue, and what was written in the email chains, the team was able to explore what members proposed to each other, and how this was recognized and acknowledged in subsequent responses (Bloome, Carter, Christian, Otto, & Shuart-Faris, 2005). Guided by these conceptual arguments, team members in different configurations[3] began a process of analyses by tracing the roots of the research alliance. This analysis was undertaken to make visible the reason leading to SCLU invitation to the interactional ethnographers to work with him, and the reason that the educational ethnographers viewed this invitation as potentially affording them an opportunity to further their understandings of teaching–learning relationships in innovative educational programmes in higher education.

To examine these roots, we began by identifying and analysing the historical chain of email exchanges (January 2012–present) initiated by SCLU. This initial data set focused on exploring what was proposed, in what ways, and for what purposes by the authors of particular messages. Table 1 provides a reconstruction of the dialogic chain of emails that constituted the initial phases of the formation of the *research alliance*. The columns represent the actors in the order in which they entered into this developing process; the cells (reading across the rows) represent responses to emails received or to whom such emails were sent.

As indicated in Table 1, SCLU initiated the process after a visit to the National Science Foundation, where he met a program officer, familiar with JLG's interest and past ethnographic work with engineering educators. The NSF program officer introduced SCLU to JLG through email, and this led to a series of email exchanges between SCLU (and a colleague) and JLG (and colleagues) that were then analysed to uncover the reasons each proposed for what this alliance might accomplish.

Through the chain of interactions in this email exchange, SCLU and JLG made visible conceptual and epistemological perspectives that they were bringing to the proposed collaboration. Analysis of this exchange led to the identification of common or intersecting interests (e.g. design thinking, exploring teaching–learning relationships and how people learn). The analysis also led to the identification of unanticipated understandings arising from the dialogues and articles exchanged as indicated in the following statement by SCLU: "It is amazing for me to know that our work in collaborative engineering has so much relevance to your interest in understanding how people learn." JLG's response to this exchange, inscribed in her email to colleagues, added to SCLU's growing awareness by proposing what her team would potentially learn, not only about what students needed to know, understand and do in this NDE course (the initial interest of the interactional ethnographers) but also what team members would learn about design thinking in engineering and its potential to frame new ways of thinking about designing for education. This analysis also revealed that SCLU and JLG viewed research alliance as a team endeavour that would lead to new understandings of what counted as the NDE approach.

Table 1. Interactive/dialogic roots of the research alliance.

SCLU	JLG
Dear JLG, I am an engineering faculty who is interested in education. Since I am no expert in education research, I could really benefit from working with people like you who study education. We have a very interesting education initiative, called NDE, which I would like to have an opportunity to introduce to you. When will be the best time for me to call? I look forward to talking with you soon.	**Dear SCLU,** I would enjoy talking with you and explore NDE with you and explore how we might work with you. We (BY and I) have been working with KB and colleagues in Engineering Education on a series of grants. We provide the social science and education research base to their studies and innovation initiatives. We also are exploring how education research can inform the design on studies of innovative practices. I will be happy to share more with you after we connect. SH (NSF officer) shared some of your work and I am intrigued with what you are doing And how you are building innovative educational processes in engineering Education. Can we connect next week on Thursday afternoon or Friday?
To JLG: PS: if it is okay with you, I would like to invite my colleague, Prof. DS, to join our conversation. Please let me know. **Sent by SCLU** to JLG – (See in references): Jing and Lu (2010), Lu (2008).	**To SCLU:** Great. I look forward to speaking with you and DS. I would like to invite two colleagues also, BY who is Executive Director of our Center. She is co-PI on engineering education grants we have submitted with colleagues at UState. I am not certain that they can join but I wanted to introduce you to them also. I see a lot of potential intersecting interests. Would you be able to send me copies of some of your papers? I tried to locate some of the journals on our ejournals but I was not able to do that. Thank you in advance for sharing these. I think that these are central to work we are doing and I want to explore how they intersect with our work exploring how in and through discourse in time and over time, participants in educational contexts socially negotiate what counts as learning, identity, and disciplinary knowledge. We have developed ways of representing this complex set of processes and different levels of analytic scale. Most of our work is published in research volumes but one that might be of interest is a comparative study that is not ethnography but shows some of our logic that might be of interest. **Sent to SCLU:** Castanheira et al. (2000)
Hi JLG: We are excited by the perspective of working with you on our common interest. It is amazing for me to know that our work in collaborative engineering has so much relevance to your interest in understanding how people learn. As promised, I will get back to you later regarding the specifics of how we may be able to work together.	**To members of the LINC Center;** Check out the Structure of argument paper. I see his framework for design engineering as having a potential for helping school leaders and systems develop ways of designing possible ways of (re)designing educational opportunities at the classroom, school as well as individual level. His work and his model(s) provide a new language and related actions and activity processes that can help build a new systems approach to (re) formulating educational possibilities in STEM and more generally for the work in Education. This has the potential to frame an integrated approach to systemic change designs with multiple actors, interdependent systems, and systems of accountability.

Rich points as anchors for tracing roots, understandings and actions taken

The analysis presented above served as an anchor for examining further exchanges for instances in which SCLU and JLG (and their team members) (1) proposed ways that the alliance was developing, (2) framed challenges they were experiencing in working dialogically and (3) identified actions necessary to further develop their understandings of key concepts raised by the other. In this section, we focus on multiple *rich points* (Agar, 1995, 2006) that were constructed as anchors for exploring intertextual references (Bloome & Egan-Robertson, 1993; Fairclough, 1992) related to discursive work in each of these areas. Building on Bloome et al. (2005), we conceptualized each rich point identified as an anchor for tracing instances of intertextually tied references to particular actions, meanings and events that members recognized as significant to understanding their point of view on a particular phenomenon.

Underlying the concept of rich points are theoretical arguments from anthropology and studies of language-in-use/discourse-in-use. Anthropologist Michael Agar (1995, 2006) argues that a *rich point* is created when an ethnographer (or by extension, a participant) wonders what is happening, or seeks to understand what others mean, or are proposing. At such points, the ethnographer (and by extension, the conversational partner) wonders about what led to or framed the phenomena in question, and what knowledge and understandings were needed to discuss that phenomena in ways that the other could understand. As indicated previously, Agar argued that at such points *culture happens*; that is when *clashes in frames of reference* or understandings occur (Gee & Green, 1998; Gumperz & Tannen, 1979), a potential is created for exploring further the insider cultural knowledge and understandings. Once a *frame clash* is identified, as will be demonstrated, it can be turned into anchors (rich points) for further analysis. Rich points, therefore, are constructions by the analyst to anchor different levels of analysis in order to uncover the roots of challenges to understanding experienced by particular members, thus making visible what had been previously unknown (see *telling case* in next section).

Central to understanding the value of rich points is Agar's (2006) arguments that ethnographers enter a *languaculture* (*LC2*) and draw on their own languaculture (*LC1*) to read and interpret what is being socially (discursively) constructed or is required of members of the social group. He argued that language is imbued with culture, that culture is realized through language and that the two are interdependent. Building on this argument, we view members of each discipline in our research alliance as constituting different *languacultures* as well as the developing course, *and* the alliance itself, as developing *languacultures*. (See Baker & Däumer this volume, for a complementary discussion.)

This argument supports the need to explore not only how, if and in what ways the potential conceptual intersections *referenced* (inscribed by authors) in the initiating chain of emails (Table 1) were taken up and continued (or not) in subsequent chains of interaction but also the conceptual arguments presented in the published texts that were exchanged. Therefore, the next step in analysis involved identifying how each author (or set of authors) defined key constructs, and which constructs were unique to a discipline as well as which were potentially common to both disciplines. This analysis engaged members of both the engineering group and the interactional ethnographers in identifying key constructs across these texts, thus creating opportunities to explore both insider knowledge of key constructs and constructs "potentially" similar in meaning (see Table 2).

As indicated in the centre column, a convergence was identified for four areas: the social construction of everyday life, how actors bring past histories to this process and how studying this process involves a nonlinear, abductive approach. This contrastive approach identified potential areas of convergence as well as differences in

Table 2. Inscriptions of concepts in exchanged articles.

SCLU: Jing and Lu (2010) – Lu (2008)	Common constructs	JLG: Castanheira et al. (2000)
Constructivism and constructionism are identical (Lu, 2008, p. 3).	*Meaning as social construction*	From a constructionism perspective, artifacts are created through social interactions (p.354 and p. 395).
Cultures are inscribed and given, and are mainly about national/ethnical culture (Jing & Lu, 2010, p. 726).	*Culture shapes social practice; Social practice is situated within a context*	Culture is socially constructed (p. 354); Culture-in-the-making and culture can be created within any given group of people (p. 394).
Reasoning as a progressive and deductive process (Lu, 2008, p. 3).	*Reasoning is an iterative process*	The iterative research process enabled us to examine a range of cultural practices and to explore how these practices, in turn, shaped what is being accomplished interactionally (p. 358).
Engineering designers "must synthesize various social, economic, and technical factors to create purposeful and functional artifacts that can satisfy customer needs and sustain market competition" (Lu, 2008, p. 1).		Reasoning as a recursive, non-linear and abductive process (p. 358).
"…[engineering] design practice is always goal driven and occurs within some social contexts as boundary conditions" (Lu, 2008, p. 7).	*Individuals' backgrounds, perspectives, viewpoints, and values figure into their actions*	"…literacy is socially constructed phenomenon that is situationally defined and redefined within and across differing social groups…" (p. 354).
"The long-term goal of our research is to develop scientific understandings of synthesis reasoning for it to be systematically taught at universities" (Lu, 2008, p. 22).		The overarching question is: "How can we understand the ways in which literate practices are shaped, and in turn shape, the everyday events of classroom life, and thus, the opportunities that [students] had for learning?"(p. 357).

understandings that members brought to ongoing dialogues. As the analysis in the next section will show, although there were points of intersection, each team had a particular understanding of common phenomena that raised potential challenges for alliance members to develop transdisciplinary understandings of particular phenomena central to understanding teaching–learning processes in common ways.

Illustrative example of a rich point and point of intersection

In Table 3, we examine a rich point (a frame clash) that was created when SCLU responded to an observation that JLG shared with him during a Google Hangout meeting.

INTERDISCIPLINARY AND INTERCULTURAL PROGRAMMES

Table 3. Analysis of challenges inscribed by SCLU.

Topic set	Inscribed understandings by paragraph	Actions and challenges inscribed by SCLU
Paragraph 1		
1	• Your comment of constantly switching the roles between an ethnographer and a student is interesting to me.	Framing actions taken by ethnographers as a point for further exploration
2	• My laymen understanding is that an ethnographer tries to understand the "context" of what a subject is doing while a student is mostly interested in learning the "content" of how to do things as a subject.	Identifying perception of ethnographer's roles – focus on context not content
3	• Since I believe that an innovator must know the content and the context of a hidden demand, • I have tried to teach my students both in this course.	Defining what constitutes the innovator's knowledge and actions
4	• That may be a reason for the sometime confusing focuses on them	Framing possible consequences of his actions for students
5	• I believe that, unlike contents, which can be taught in classrooms, contexts can only be learned among each other; • and the best way to acquire both is to do them iteratively	Contrasting teaching of content with learning as contextual and iterative
6	• However, trying to do both in one class is challenging because targeting the development of contextual understanding as a learning objective really challenges the traditional pedagogy of classroom lecturing of contents.	Framing challenges of doing both as challenge to traditional pedagogy
7	• Not knowing how to achieve this learning objective exactly and not having an established body of knowledge to "learn to teach", I often find myself doing the "teach to learn" experiment. • Therefore, I also feel that often times I find myself switching the roles between a teacher and a student with this [NDE] course.	Framing limits to knowledge of how to "learn to teach" in new way to achieve goals and take action: *switching roles between teacher and student*
Paragraph 2		
8	• Because of this alternating role between student and teacher, I am unable to always give definite answers to your following six questions. • During the days when I feel like a teacher, I can think of many good answers to these questions without difficulties; • but during the time when I feel more like a student, I become very unsure about if I know anything about cross-cultural learning. • I guess today is the latter – therefore, I will have to wait to another day to try to answer these questions.	Identifying feelings associated with switching roles between teaching and being a student in way that makes visible a dialectical process in exploring teaching and studenting relationships

(Continued)

Table 3. (*Continued*).

Topic set	Inscribed understandings by paragraph	Actions and challenges inscribed by SCLU
Paragraph 3		
9	• But I do want to make an attempt here to respond to your last question: "How is your approach to design thinking guiding your approach to designing your course?"	Shifting focus to address a question on the role of design thinking in relationship to course
10	• I find this question interesting and important because, after all, I must convince people that I can talk my talk and walk my walk, right? • (BTW, until an American friend corrected me a few years ago, I used to say that I should "walk my talk" because I always thought that one should be able to do (i.e., walk or take action) what he/she thinks (i.e., talk or wish for)).	Linking his view of design thinking to his actions in designing course and programme
11	• What a good example of cultural learning! [indent in original].	Linking what he learned from colleague to concept of cultural learning

This response did not occur during the meeting but through an email (7 March 2012) in which SCLU inscribed a series of challenges that occurred for him within the dialogues. Underlying this analysis is a conceptual argument by critical discourse analyst Norman Fairclough (1992) that each utterance (written or spoken) is three things – a text, a discourse practice and a social process, and that there are traces of other texts in a developing text.

This argument framed a three-step analytic process. The first step involved using the paragraph structure that SCLU inscribed in the email (i.e. three paragraphs). Each paragraph was placed in a cell in the left column, and sentences or clusters of sentences (topic sets) constituting the topic were identified. In this way, we constructed an analytic text to examine how SCLU inscribed his understandings of his own thinking in relationship to that of the ethnographers as well as students. To analyse the topic sets he inscribed, we created an action column to explore the social processes implicated in the actions identified. Actions were represented as present continuous verb plus object of the action, given the linguistic argument that *English is a subject-verb-object language*; thus, by adding the objects of the actions identified, we were able to explore the purpose of the actions he inscribed. By tying each action to a particular segment of a paragraph, we also identified a link between what he referred to and context of interpretation of the social actions and objects inscribed.

As indicated in Table 3, although what JLG said to SCLU in a Google Hangout conversation was not visible, in his email SCLU inscribed a bit from this conversation when he identified what was 'intriguing' to him – "Your comment of constantly switching the roles between an ethnographer and a student is interesting to me." Analysis of his responses in topic sets on 8–11 revealed a series of ongoing conceptual challenges he argued faced innovators as well as students. In topic set 8, he directly explored the shifting roles involved in learning from his teaching and the personal consequences of shifting from the position of teacher to one of student. He also provided an explanation of why he could not directly answer JLG's question. In the final two topics, he once again shifted his focus to identify a question that was raised by JLG – "How is your approach to design thinking guiding your approach to designing your course?" Although he did not answer the question in this email, he marked it as *interesting and important* to consider in the future in relationship to the challenges he was facing in what he viewed as a *"teaching to learn" experiment*. His stance towards learning through teaching, and the alliance dialogue, was further articulated in his example of how he elicited and developed what he called *cultural learning* (topic set 11).

The action column provided a basis for identifying reflexive actions that SCLU (and by extension, the ethnographers) were engaged in as they observed or planned for instruction as well as engaged in dialogues about the complex nature of understanding each other's insider perspectives. The following argument by Mikhail Bakhtin (1986) captures ways of understanding the challenges that SCLU inscribed as well as those facing the ethnographers in uncovering what counts as NDE. Bakhtin argued,

> Sooner or later what is heard and actively understood will find its response in the subsequent speech or behavior of the listener. In most cases, genres of complex cultural communication are intended precisely for this kind of actively responsive understanding with delayed action. Everything that we have said here also pertains to written and read speech, with the appropriate adjustments and additions. (p. 60)

In the rich point, SCLU not only inscribed elements of overtime work needed to develop understandings of teacher–student relationships undertaken to meet his goals of constructing innovative learning opportunities for students, he also inscribed why responses to questions posed by different actors in the alliance required time and further consideration. Bakhtin's argument also makes visible why this (or any) approach to designing as well as researching complex processes that constitute teaching–learning relationships requires exploring developing understandings of different actors, that is, those creating the innovative teaching–learning processes as well as the research team seeking emic understanding of the developing processes.

Part 2: From rich points to telling cases

In this section, we present a series of ethnographic analyses that formed the basis of *telling cases* that made visible an unanticipated set of challenges the ethnographers encountered in identifying factors central to understanding what counted as the NDE approach. The first two analyses constitute *telling cases* (Mitchell, 1984) of the layers or actions that SCLU undertook in designing and engaging students in the NDE course. Guiding the analyses in the first two cases is a conceptual argument that the course was an ongoing construction by participants in and outside of the class itself and that to explore what counted as NDE, the content and the expected actions of participants, analyses need to identify intertextually and historically tied events (c.f., Bloome & Egan-Robertson, 1993; Bloome et al., 2005). Case 1, therefore, examines the actions taken by particular actors located in three national universities (US, China and Taiwan) to select students for this course. Case 2 shifts the focus from actions external to the moments of instruction to an exploration of how SCLU engaged students in and across cycles of intertextually tied events, each focusing on particular areas of the course. Case 3 shifts the angle of analysis from the course to an analysis of conceptual transformations of members of the alliance that SCLU and his team proposed to the ethnographers, and how, in turn, the table that

SCLU and his team created to record these transformations became an anchor for exploring what SCLU and his team viewed as fundamental phenomena in conceptualizing teaching–learning processes.

Defining telling cases

Anthropologist Clyde Mitchell (1984) frames a telling case as one in which "the events themselves may relate to any level of social organization: a whole society, some section of a community, a family or an individual" (p. 238). He frames a telling case in terms, not only of events, but also in terms of times and actors. He argued that rather than focus on a single event, or restricted set of events in the same situation, the ethnographer constructs telling cases by tracing an individual (or group) across extended periods of time. This process he argued allows "the analyst to present material which contributes historical or dynamic dimension to the account", and that each case is treated "as a stage in an ongoing process of social relations between specific persons and groups in a social system or culture" (p. 239).

Mitchell further argued that through such cases ethnographers *construct inferences* based on the "*theoretical* relationships among conceptually defined elements in the sample" (p. 241), and that theoretical inferences are based on *analytic induction*. From this perspective, a "telling" case is one "in which the particular circumstances surrounding a case, serve to make previously obscure theoretical relationships suddenly apparent". Additionally he argued that "the particularity of the circumstances surrounding any case or situation (or set of situations) must always be located within some wider setting or context" (p. 241). This argument guided the logic-in-use (Birdwhistell, 1977) the selection of cases as well as their construction.

Telling case 1: tracing the historical roots of NDE

The first telling case examines challenges facing the interactional ethnographers in understanding who the different actors were that were involved in both designing the course and recruiting/selected students for this course (case 1). This telling case, therefore, explores the layers of actors and their decisions and actions they undertook to create the infrastructure of the NDE initiative, and the course on *Principles and Practices of Global Innovation*. Figure 1 is a graphic (re)construction of the historical actions of the cycles of activity they engaged in to construct the NDE courses (2010–2012); therefore, Figure 1 represents a macro-level analysis of the structuring processes taken by members of the participating institutions in this particular iteration of the NDE course taught by SCLU.

As indicated in Figure 1, 2012 was the third iteration of the NDE course with the same three international partners: US University (USU), China University (CNU) and Taiwan University (TWU). As represented in this figure, the process began with a process of recruiting and interviewing students. However, what is not (re)presented are the disciplines of the students recruited, a fact that posed a challenge to the ethnographers, since that level of information was not visible in actions among members. To obtain this information, a request was sent by the ethnographic team to AL, the TA for the course, who resolved the problem by retrieving the following data: USU recruited engineering and business students, and CNU and TWU recruited students in engineering, social science, science and the humanities. He also identified that in 2012, 60 students were

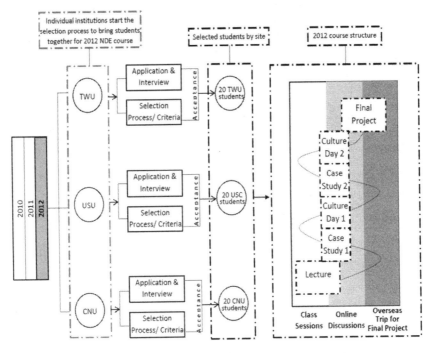

Figure 1. Historical (re)construction of course in larger programme contexts.

selected, with 20 enrolled in each university and that each university had an instructor of record as well as a teaching assistant.

Also indicated in Figure 1 is the general structure that students engaged in as the course developed across times and events. This structure made visible a series of recursive cycles of activity (Green et al., 2012) that constituted fundamental areas for learning global innovations and design thinking with cross-national colleagues: lectures, case studies ($n = 2$) and cultures projects ($n = 2$). These cycles of activity involved multiple spaces for interaction: face-to-face, online discussions and travel oversees for final projects.

This telling case revealed layers of epistemological and institutional decisions and timelines of actions constructed by a complex web of actors. This case also made visible the range of data constructed and analysed in order to develop this (re)construction of the course structure and participants. Data construction included analysis of information on the iPodia website; collaborative work with AL to retrieve invisible layers of decisions; and virtual observations in class as it developed as well as historical knowledge that DY, a doctoral student researcher, provided based on her history with different iterations of this course: as a student (2010), a teaching assistant (2011) and as a coordinator (2012) at CNU. Through this process, therefore, members of engineering education team supported the ethnographers, creating situated opportunities for dialogues that added depth to this (re)presentation would not have been possible by observations alone.

Telling case 2: structuring as a culturally responsive process

The question of factors supporting, and/or constraining, how SCLU structured the course, in and across times and events (20 weeks), required further levels of analysis, each

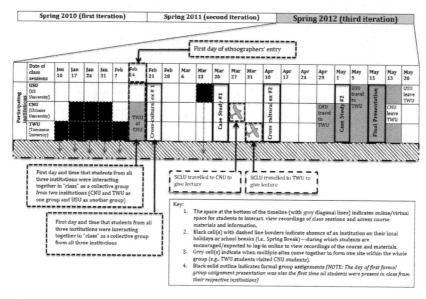

Figure 2. Structuring cycles of learning.

focusing on particular levels of context, when and where recursive cycles of subject matter were located and who participated in which sessions. This approach to analysis drew on research on teaching–learning relationships as constructed across times and events (e.g. Baker, Green, & Skukauskaite, 2008; Castanheira et al., 2000; Kelly & Chen, 1999).

Figure 2 provides a graphic (re)presentation of multiple levels of analysis undertaken to uncover unanticipated dimensions of the structuring processes, for example, different starting points for students (and the ethnographers) in the course related to differences in cultural and institutional policies and practices across national contexts.

As indicated in Figure 2, USU students entered the first week of the course. In contrast, CNU students attended the first and fifth week, but not week 24, and TWU did not attend the first five weeks. In an interview, SCLU explained that these differences were related to the weeks of the Chinese New Year celebrations, which were institutional holidays. TWU and CNU students were given the option of attending from home through virtual links and/or to engage with video records of these sessions in an online repository. Additionally, USU students had a holiday (week 13), while CNU and TWU students met with SCLU, who travelled first to CNU and then to TWU. Additionally, SCLU conducted sessions from each of these international sites, with USU students attending from home (March 27) and then in class (March 31). This process afforded students in international sites opportunities to work with SCLU face-to-face, and USU students to experience the virtual dimension of this course in new ways. Finally, as indicated in Figure 2, students (faculty and TA's) in CNU and USU travelled, at the end of the course, to TWU to engage face-to-face with their partners on their final projects.

Analysis of who attended when, or did not attend particular course sessions, revealed structuring processes that are often invisible in studies that focus primarily on the interactions of teachers with students in a course session. Analysis of the responsive structuring process also revealed challenges in inter-institutional coordination, the need for making class sessions available after the face-to-face sessions and how times for learning differed based on local institutional and cultural events that impacted when instruction could be made available to students. The analysis also revealed that, like students at CNU and TWU, the ethnographers entered the course in the sixth week, February 21, and faced challenges of understanding what had occurred with the USU students.

By tracing actors across times and events, and by contrasting who had access to which cycles of activity within and across time, we were able to identify the complex and developing nature of the course as well as the challenges facing SCLU and his team in meeting the different institutional and cultural practices as he sought to engage students in this NDE course. This analysis also demonstrated that understanding the design of this course required uncovering multiple levels of structuring and the purposes of each. It also made visible the importance of exploring historical decisions involved in structuring for global interactions among students. This telling case, therefore, made visible why analysis of teaching–learning relationships in a particular course requires examination of multiple time frames and angles of analysis, thus challenging the dominant view that effective teaching or learning is possible by direct observations in particular moments in a developing course.

Telling case 3: on how understandings were reformulated and new actions taken

In this section, we present one final telling case. This case returns to an exploration of how these dialogues and analyses created opportunities for the ethnographers to learn about what SCLU and his team gained through the dialogues, and research processes developed jointly by alliance members. Table 4 was constructed by SCLU's team in response to the question from the ethnographers: *So what did you gain by inviting our ethnographic team?*

The transformational processes inscribed in this table were often unanticipated ones for both teams. However, once identified, they made visible layers of work (e.g. tracing of theoretical arguments undertaken, reformulating assignments) that were not visible during the dialogues at particular points in time. What SCLU's team made visible was how the dialogues, like his experiments in learning from teaching, became opportunities for exploring differences the language used by each team about teaching–learning relationships. By sharing how their team viewed points of transformation leading to (re)consideration of actions they took, SCLU and his team constructed opportunities for the ethnographers to (re)examine points of convergence and difference in understandings. Although this table of transformational processes was unanticipated, it made visible the mutual exploration of theory–practice–understanding relationships and how these were constructed across time in and through the dialogues and actions taken by members of the research alliance.

A closing and an opening

This study explored how a research alliance created opportunities for members to (re)examine fundamental conceptual arguments individually and collectively, along with epistemological processes necessary to uncover the often-invisible levels of design decisions underlying the development of innovative global programmes and courses in higher education. It also demonstrated why multiple levels of analyses were critical in developing grounded understandings of the complex nature of teaching and learning

Table 4. Transforming understandings from the engineering team's perspective.

	SCLU and AL's (A team member) inscription of chains of transformed understandings				JLG's (and team) developing understandings of role of dialogues
Topic	Initial assumptions	Transformed understandings	Transformed actions		What conceptual transformations made visible
Constructivism and contructionism	Design is a social construction process but we failed to distinguish between social constructivism and social constructionism.	Social constructionism focuses on the artefacts that are created through the social interactions of a group, while social constructivism focuses on an individual's learning that takes place because of their interactions in a group.	Social constructionism can be regarded as the foundation of collaborative design, where the focus lies in the artefacts being created – team project. Social constructivism is the foundation of studying how students learn from each other via peer-peer interactions.		SCLU and AL's actions to differentiate between constructionism and constructivism, making visible the need to explore often-invisible theoretical goals of SCLU as an engineering educator.
Culture as national-bordered	Our past interpretation of cultural was very limited. For example, we used to characterize cultures merely from the national perspective – American, Chinese and Taiwanese cultures.	The class developed an exclusive no-distance teaching/learning culture and the project teams developed a multi-cultural virtual collaboration culture.			Take up of dialogues on conceptual view of classes as cultures-in-the-making, and how these led to (re) consideration of what counts as culture.
Teaching as an iterative and progressive process	SCLU's teaching developed in an iterative manner, for example, the same concept/principles is repeated in different scenarios… SCLU's teaching also developed in a progressive manner, following a gradual zoom-in process…	Together, SCLU's teaching developed in a recursive manner, repeating items in a self-similar way with increasing details or divergent contexts.	Avoid repeating the same content, instead, assign different problems to practice the same design methods both in class and after class.		Opportunities to examine basis for iterative and recursive practices during instruction in response to student understandings of proposed content as well as cultural differences in interpretation of common tasks.
Knowing how to learn	Students will naturally know or actively learn how to learn in a new no-distance learning environment.	It's important to start preparing student's mind along the whole process….	Start to prepare student's mind as early as during the student selection stage. Collecting advice from former students to future students in terms of challenges of attending this class…		Multiple point of entering the course and SCLU's use of student feedback as grounding for changing particular dimensions of course processes.

processes jointly constructed by SCLU with an interdisciplinary and transnational group of students. The dialogic research and conceptual arguments among members revealed a complex and interdependent series of angles of analysis necessary to contextualize what was available to be "seen" at particular points in time. This series revealed a web of often-invisible actors that supported the interactions among the instructor and students, and students in different countries across sessions, cycles of activity and structuring processes (Giddens, 1987). Analysis of the dialogues among alliance members led to a series of unanticipated ways in which alliance members created transdisciplinary understandings of teaching–learning relationships. These understandings often resulted from ways in which individual members made visible understandings they (re)formulated about teaching–learning relationships: concepts of culture as dynamic, constructionism–constructivism relationships and disciplinary knowledge as developing across actors, times, intercultural interactions and events. The dialogues also made visible the need to examine institutional, discipline-based and interpersonal dimensions of processes involved in designing intercultural/interdisciplinary opportunities for learning with global participants. Together, the telling cases and analyses of the developing dialogues demonstrated the importance of exploring how content/subject matter(s) are contextually bounded as well as intertextually constructed with participants in differing configurations of actors, times, spaces and goals, creating inter-transdisciplinary opportunities for learning global innovation processes.

Notes

1. For historical volumes exploring what can be learned through interdisciplinary explorations of how different conceptual traditions shape what can be known about teaching–learning processes in classrooms as well as factors supporting and/or constraining learning, see Cazden, John, and Hymes (1972), Green and Harker (1988), Wyatt-Smith, Elkins, and Gunn (2011) and Guzzetti and Hynds (1998).
2. For the remaining sections of the paper, we use the initials of the different actors, SCLU, AL (postdoctoral scholar), JLG (the educational ethnographer) and NSF as a basis for stepping back from ethnocentrism. This approach focuses on exploring the actors in the dialogues through their words and actions that were inscribed in the texts constructed and exchanged or made available to other members.
3. Although the interactional ethnographic team took the lead on this angle of analysis, the engineering team members were instrumental in identifying necessary data for the analysis – for example, insider perspectives on a particular phenomena, student records, decisions made as well as actions taken in designing for instruction in the virtual spaces, and records of student collaborations across national borders. This process, therefore, like the email and face-to-face dialogues, created unanticipated opportunities to identify actions involved in exploring phenomena of mutual interest.

References

Agar, M. (1995). *Language shock: Understanding the culture of conversation*. New York, NY: William Morrow.

Agar, M. (2006). An ethnography by any other name: In *Forum qualitative sozialforschung/forum: Qualitative Social Research* (ISSN 1438-5627), 7(4). Retrieved from http://www.qualitative-research.net/fqs/

Baker, W. D., Green, J. L., & Skukauskaite, A. (2008). Video-enabled ethnographic research: A microethnographic perspective. In R. F. Ellen (Ed.), *How to do educational ethnography* (pp. 76–114). London: Tufnell.

Bakhtin, M. M. (Ed.). (1986). Speech genres and other late essays. In *Speech genres and other late essays* (pp. 60–102). Austin: University of Texas.

Birdwhistell, R. L. (Ed.). (1977). Some discussion of ethnography, theory and method. In *About Bateson: Essays on Gregory Bateson* (pp. 103–144). London: Wildwood.

Bloome, D., Carter, S. P., Christian, B. M., Otto, S., & Shuart-Faris, N. (2005). *Discourse analysis and the study of classroom language and literacy events: A microethnographic perspective.* London: Routledge.

Bloome, D., & Egan-Robertson, A. (1993). The social construction of intertextuality in classroom reading and writing lessons. *Reading Research Quarterly 28*(4), 434–462.

Castanheira, M. L., Crawford, T., Dixon, C. N., & Green, J. L. (2000). Interactional ethnography: An approach to studying the social construction of literate practices. *Linguistics and Education, 11*(4), 353–400. doi:10.1016/S0898-5898(00)00032-2

Cazden, C. B., John, V. P., & Hymes, D. (1972). *Functions of language in the classroom.* New York and London: Teachers College.

Fairclough, N. (1992). Discourse and text: Linguistic and intertextual analysis within discourse analysis. *Discourse & Society, 3*(2), 193–217. doi:10.1177/0957926592003002004

Gee, J. P., & Green, J. L. (1998). Discourse analysis, learning, and social practice: A methodological study. *Review of Research in Education, 23*, 119–169.

Giddens, A. (1987). *Social theory and modern sociology.* Oxford: Polity.

Green, J. L., & Harker, J. O. (Eds.). (1988). *Multidisciplinary perspectives on classroom discourse.* Norwood, NJ: Ablex.

Green, J. L., Skukauskaite, A., & Baker, W. D. (2012). Ethnography as epistemology. In J. Arthur, M. I. Waring, R. Coe, & L. V. Hedges (Eds.), *Research methods and methodologies in education* (pp. 309–321). New York, NY: SAGE Publications.

Gumperz, J. J., & Tannen, D. (1979). Individual and social differences in language use. In C. Fillmore, D. Kempler, & W. Wang (Eds.), *Individual differences in language ability.* New York, NY: Academic.

Guzzetti, B., & Hynd, C. (Eds.). (1998). *Perspectives on conceptual change: Multiple ways to understand knowing and learning in a complex world.* Mahwah, NJ: Lawrence Erlbaum Associates.

Heap, J. (1991). A situated perspective on what counts as reading. In C. Baker & A. Luke (Eds.), *Towards a critical sociology of reading pedagogy* (pp. 103–139). Amsterdam: John Benjamins.

Heap, J. (1995). The status of claims in "qualitative" educational research. *Curriculum Inquiry, 25*(3), 271–292. doi:10.2307/1179908

Heath, S. B. (1982). Ethnography in education: defining the essentials. In P. Gilmore & A. Glatthorn (Eds.), *Children in and out of school: Ethnography and education* (pp. 35–55). Washington, DC: Center for Applied Linguistics.

Jing, N., & Lu, S. C.-Y. (2010). Structure arguments for collaborative negotiation of group decisions in manufacturing systems integration. *International Journal of Computer Integrated Manufacturing, 23*(8–9), 720–738. doi:10.1080/09511921003730819

Kelly, G. J., & Chen, C. (1999). The sound of music: Constructing science as sociocultural practices through oral and written discourse. *Journal of Research in Science Teaching, 36*(8), 883–915. doi:10.1002/(SICI)1098-2736(199910)36:8<883::AID-TEA1>3.0.CO;2-I

Lima, E. S. (1995). Culture revisited: Vygotsky's ideas in Brazil. *Anthropology & Education Quarterly, 26*(4), 443–457.

Lu, S. C.-Y. (2008). *A theory of synthesis reasoning for engineering design.* Working paper. Los Angeles, CA: Department of Engineering Education, Vertibi School of Engineering, USC.

Mitchell, J. C. (1984). Typicality and the case study. In R. F. Ellen (Ed.), *Ethnographic research: A guide to general conduct* (pp. 238–241). New York, NY: Academic.

National Academies of Sciences, Engineering & Institutes of Medicine. (2004). *Facilitating interdisciplinary research.* Washington, DC: The National Academies.

Strike, K. A. (1989). *Liberal justice and the Marxist critique of education: A study of conflicting research programs.* New York, NY: Routledge.

Swiss Academy of Arts and Sciences. (2014). *Transdisciplinary research: The plurality of definitions.* Retrieved from: http://www.transdisciplinarity.ch/e/Transdisciplinarity/TRdefinitions.php

Wyatt-Smith, C., Elkins, J., & Gunn, S. (Eds.). (2011). *Multiple perspectives on difficulties in learning literacy and numeracy.* New York, NY: Springer Publishers.

Index

Note: **Boldface** page numbers refer to figures and tables, page numbers followed by "n" denote endnotes

Academic Literacies (AcLits) approach 71–2
academic writing 70–1; Academic Literacies approach 71–2; Angolan and Campo students' context 72–3; Campo (Rural) Pedagogy Program 72; extended analysis of Campo students 80–2; interviews with non-traditional students 73–4; matrix features of 74, **75**; Portuguese language as contested terrain 74–7; positioning 78–9
AcLits approach *see* Academic Literacies approach
ACTFL *see* American Association of Teachers of Foreign Languages
Agar, Michael 7, 9–10, 40, 41, 58–9, 91
American Association of Teachers of Foreign Languages (ACTFL) 7
analytic induction 2, 96
Angolan students: academic writing style 74–9; in Brazilian universities 72–3; interviews and observations 73–4; matrix features of writing 74, **75**; Portuguese language as contested terrain 74–7; positioning 78–9

Bakhtin, Mikhail 95
Baumann, Zygmut 31
blended intercultural model 6
Blue Ribbon Panel 56
Brazilian linguistic market 75–7
Brazilian universities: academic writing of non-traditional students *see* academic writing; Angolan and Campo students in 72–3
Byram, Michael 11

CALL *see* computer-assisted language learning
Campo students: academic writing style 80–2; in Brazilian universities 72–3; Campo (Rural) Pedagogy Program 72; interviews and observations 73–4

Camtasia™ screen capture 25, 26
China University (CNU) 96, **97**, 98–9
China-USA Business Café (CUBC) project 14, 16
"closed-loop" design 25
CMapTools™ 23
CMC *see* computer-mediated communication
CNU *see* China University
cognitive theories 8, 9
College of Arts and Sciences 42
"communicative competence" 7; *see also* intercultural communicative competence
computer-assisted language learning (CALL) 10
computer-mediated communication (CMC) 15
concept mapping 23
conflicting institutional expectations: data collection 60–1; elementary field placement 60; field-based actors' perspectives 61, 63; implications 66–7; languacultures 65–6; lesson planning and teaching 58, 61, **62–3**; overview of 54–5; paradigm conceptualization 56; principles of operation 58–9; program contexts and actors 59–60; supervisor's perspective 63–5; supervisory practices at intersection 56–8; teacher education program 60, 67
CUBC project *see* China-USA Business Café project
Cultura model 12; in global context 13–14; meta-synthesis of 12–13; word associations and sentence completions in 13, 21

Darling-Hammond, L. 55
discipline-based scholarship 39–40

Early Childhood Teacher Licensing Program 59
English Education faculty 42
e-tandem model 6
expressive potential 2–3, 3n2, 58

"failed communication" 15
Filipino Heritage Language Café 14, 16
"flexible knowledge", notion of 31–2

INDEX

foreign language/second language (FL/SL) telecollaboration 5, 6; blended intercultural model 6; competence and e-literacies 7; *Cultura* model 12–14; e-tandem model 6; goal of 7; INTENT project 6, 11; intercultural communicative competence 6, 7; for language and culture learning 8; limitations and invisible constraints in 15–17; methodologies for researching 10–11; second language acquisition *see* second language acquisition; sociocultural theory 6–7

ICC *see* intercultural communicative competence
IE *see* interactional ethnographic approach
INTENT project 11
interactional ethnographic (IE) approach 27, 43, 101n3
intercultural communicative competence (ICC) 5, 7; development of **8**; in higher education 6; second language acquisition 9–10
interdisciplinary dialogues 86–7, 99, 101, 101n1, 101n3; frame clash 91; guiding questions and conceptual approach 87; languacultures 91; rich points, concept of 91–2, **92–4**, 94–5; stepping back from ethnocentrism 88–9, **90**; telling cases *see* telling cases; theoretical/conceptual arguments 87–8
interdisciplinary instruction: classroom events 44–50, **46–8**; discipline-based scholarship 39–40; ethnographic perspective 43–4; in higher education 40–2; increased reflexivity 44; layers of context 42–3; overview of 38–9

languaculture (LC): Agar's concept of 7, 40, 58–9, 91; disciplines/disciplinarity as 39, 51; frame clashes 65
learning management system (LMS) 23
Linguistic Inquiry and Word Count (LIWC) 11
'logic-in-use' 1–3, 59, 88

MCC *see* multimodal communicative competence
Mitchell, J. C. 2, 44, 96
Modern Language Association (MLA) 7
multimodal communicative competence (MCC) 8

National Council for Accreditation of Teacher Education (NCATE) 56
NDE approach *see* no distance education approach
New Literacy Studies (NLS) 71
no distance education (NDE) approach 87, 96–7, **97**

online intercultural exchange (OIE) 5–6, 10, 15, 16
"Outstanding Teaching Award (Team)" 23

PBL curriculum *see* problem-based learning curriculum
Portuguese language, as contested terrain 74–7
positioning theory 78–9
Praxis III: Classroom Performance Assessments 60
Prince Cinders (Cole) 45
Principles and Practices of Global Innovation 87, 96
problem-based learning (PBL) curriculum: cascade searching 30; characteristics of 23; closed-loop/reiterative problem design 25; in dental education 24; digital learning materials in 33; educational objectives 25, 33; event map of major transitions **26**, 26–7; 5-year philosophy and structure 24; "flexible knowledge" 31–2; interactional ethnographic approach 26, 31; intervisual link 28, 31, 32; knowledge-building 32; materials and methods 25–6; ongoing research 34; overview of 22–3; as pedagogic approach and curriculum design 23–4, 31; problem cycle **24**, 27, 31; PubMed searching 29; Quick Time Virtual Reality study model 28, 29
problem cycle **24**, 27, 31
process-oriented research 23
programme of research 2–3
psycholinguistic theories 8, 9

Quick Time Virtual Reality (QTVR) study model 28, 29

"Reading, Interpreting and Responding to Literature" 43
reiterative problem design 25
rich points, concept of 91–2, **92–4**, 94–5

SDL *see* self-directed learning
second language acquisition (SLA): cognitive theories of 8, 9; ecological approaches 10; historical dichotomies in 8; intercultural communicative competence 9–10; psycholinguistic theories 8, 9; sociocultural theories of 9; theories and models of **8**
self-directed learning (SDL) 23, 27, 31–3
SLA *see* second language acquisition
sociocultural theory 6, 8; of second language acquisition 9
Socratic methods 23
Strike, Kenneth 2–3

INDEX

Taiwan University (TWU) 96, **97**, 98–9
telecollaboration *see* foreign language/second language telecollaboration
telling cases 2, 26; conceptualization of 96; interactional ethnographic analyses 95–6; no distance education, historical roots of 96–7, **97**; structuring cycles of learning 97–9, **98**; and transformational processes 99, **100**
TWU *see* Taiwan University

United States University (USU) 96, **97**, 98–9

van Lier, L. 10

WebCT™ 25, 27
Words at Work and Play (Heath) 83
World Wide Web 6